# Cars I Have Owned

The illustrations in this book and the cover drawing are by Debra Thiem, a free-lance artist living in Colorado Springs, Colorado.

# CARS I HAVE OWNED

## and Other Financial Disasters

GLENN E. THOMPSON

THE PATRICE PRESS
TUCSON, ARIZONA

**Library of Congress Cataloging in Publication Data**

Thompson, Glenn E.
Cars I have owned and other financial disasters / Glenn E. Thompson.
p. cm.
ISBN 0-935284-98-2 : $9.95
1. Automobiles—Humor. I. Title.
PN6231.A8T46 1992
814′ .54—dc20 92-19545
CIP

**The Patrice Press**
**1810 W. Grant Rd., Suite 108**
**Tucson AZ 85745**
**1-800-367-9242**

**Printed in the United States of America**

*To Ardelle*
*who has helped me through the bad times*
*and made the good ones much more enjoyable*

# *Contents*

# *Preface*

PART OF THE REASON for writing this book is an ongoing, good natured argument with my wife, Ardelle, about my penchant for purchasing new automobiles. She is practical.

She says, "It is less expensive to keep an old car and get it fixed up, if it is basically sound of body and engine." She is right.

I say, "When you get finished with the fixing, you still have an old car whose eventual value is zero." I am right.

She says, "It is still transportation." She is right.

I say, "It may be transportation, but may not be dependable transportation." I am right.

She says, "We have spent more on cars than we have on houses." She is right.

In fact, more right than she realizes. We have owned nineteen vehicles since 1949. That averages out to one car trade every 2.263 years.

For those nineteen cars we have paid a total amount for purchase price, insurance, taxes, and maintenance of $135,365. This equals $3,148 in actual dollars per year. That doesn't sound too bad until you realize that probably half of that was in dollars worth about three to four times as much in today's purchasing power. This changes the figure to $6,500 to $7,000 per year, in 1992 dollars.

Ardelle says, "That is ridiculous." She is right.

I point out, "We wouldn't have been able to take some really enjoyable driving trips without the new cars." I am right.

From that total car outlay, we must subtract the value of the two vehicles we presently own, a 1990 three-quarter ton Suburban and a 1992 Ford Crown Victoria. Their combined value is probably less than $30,000 today. However, because we still have that value in the cars, it knocks the yearly expenditure down to less than $6,000.

I say, "You see, that makes it a lot less."

Ardelle says, "That is still too much money to pay for a car every year."

Only five of these cars were not new when purchased. Notice that there are no interest charges figured into any of the car purchases. The reason is that only the first four had car loans, and they were relatively insignificant, even when translated into today's dollars. If we had car payments, interest on the loans would have added as much as a third more to our yearly average. The $6,000 figure easily could have been $8,000 or more per year.

I say, "But we didn't finance them, therefore, look how much we have saved on cars."

It is no doubt unusual that we have not financed most of our cars during our forty years of married life. We are certainly not rich. This stems from my own conservative upbringing, and something I think is just good common sense. I won't buy a new car unless I have saved enough to pay cash for it. Otherwise, I'll purchase a used one.

Buying new is getting harder to do. I can understand why it would be particularly difficult for younger buyers who have not had time to build up savings. With the cost of new vehicles today, it may be impossible for most young families to pay cash for a car. My advice to them would be to finance a car, but to be certain it is the shortest term payment they can afford.

My figures do not include major factors in owning a car today, like gasoline, oil, and minor replacement parts, such as filters. I estimated the total figure for these necessities to be $35,250 for us over the years. Remember, gasoline was in the twenty-some cents per gallon price range during the earlier years, and that's figured in without adjustment for inflation. That $35,250 could be multiplied by at least three, if today's prices were carried back to reflect costs. Wow! That would be $105,750 for gas and oil alone.

Ardelle says, "It is absolutely unbelievable we have paid that much to operate cars."

I point out, "These costs are like monthly utility bills in our home. They are in no way involved with the actual purchase or upkeep and that is why I did not include them in average yearly car expenses."

Ardelle says, "We don't live in our car." She is right.

With all of the complicated electronics on today's cars, it really isn't practical to own the equipment required to diagnose and repair them, unless you just enjoy spending time and money fiddling around. In a few cases we did keep more simply engineered cars for a number of years. I had one for nine years back in the days when you could putter around and make a good share of repairs in your own backyard. That Model-T mentality is gone forever.

I say, "Look how much I saved us by doing my own repairs."

She says, "You don't have the right tools or a hoist. You could make a lot more money just working at your own job. You're not equipped to work on cars, and furthermore, you spent all your big savings on doctor bills when you hurt your back."

If you love working on cars, are into auto racing, or collect show cars or antiques, that's another story. Then it becomes a hobby. Many men, and an increasing number of women, enjoy an automotive hobby.

I say, "You could certainly find a lot worse hobbies."

Ardelle says, "And a lot less expensive ones."

Some people buy new cars because they like the smell of them. Since I am slightly allergic to the scent of new plastic and fabric manufactured with formaldehyde, this is the last reason I would ever buy. Deep down, I know the reason I like to own new cars is that I am fascinated with the engineering technology, which is, occasionally, a genuine improvement.

Ardelle says, "You're a car nut." She is right.

I say, "Reading, studying, and test-driving cars makes me an informed buyer." I am right.

The looks and performance of the two-door sports cars never seemed to mesh with our lifestyle at the right time. Back in my younger, single days, or even right after our marriage, a sports car would have been a perfect match.

Ardelle said, "You can't afford one."

I said, "But, if we don't buy one now, we probably never will."

The closest we ever came to owning a sports car was a seafoam green 1949 Ford two-door, just before our first child was born. Well, it was a two-door V-8 at least. After we had a family, it became obvious that only a four-door model, or station-wagon-type-truck provided the room and convenience that made sense for us. Finances were tight over a period of about twenty-five years when we were buying a home, raising children, preparing for college expenses, and purchasing cars for our three daughters. That group of six or eight used vehicles is not figured into our car expense equation, incidentally.

Then after entering the empty-nest phase, it seemed at last, we should own a sports car.

Ardelle said, "It's too hard to get groceries into them, nobody can sit in the back seat, and they ride like they've got no springs."

I said, "But think of how we could race around corners on twisty roads, the thrill of fast acceleration, and how great the car would look.''

But then, somehow, we seemed to require more luggage space. Friends traveled with us. We discovered we liked the comfort, headroom, and stretched-out feeling that is only available in a big four-door sedan. Now I am considering buying a sports car for a third vehicle. Sort of a toy for my second childhood.

Ardelle says, ''You're crazy. We can't justify the expense.''

If I do buy one, it is conceivable that I might end up writing a book about sports cars.

I say, ''You would probably divorce me if I did that.'' I am right.

—Glenn Thompson
1992

# 1

# *Romancing The Chevrolet*

IN 1949 B.C. (BEFORE CAR) I was still trying to work my way through college. At the time it wasn't particularly unusual for a twenty-year-old man's principal source of transportation to be walking. You didn't have to like it. That's just the way it was. The Constitution had not yet been amended to include the inalienable right to own a car by the age of sixteen.

Some of my youthful acquaintances owned cars. These were often people who had gone directly into the work force from high school and had full-time jobs. Others were the sons, and very rarely the daughters, of affluent families who bought cars for their offspring. Returning servicemen attending college under the GI Bill owned cars they had bought with their mustering-out pay, or with money they had saved while they were overseas.

Then there were the rest of us. I was dating a great girl

I didn't want to lose. I felt that I needed all the help possible if I was going to hold onto her. A car seemed essential. Of course, Ardelle wasn't that shallow, but what does a young college man know about women? I had observed that owning a car definitely improved one's love life. Mobility was the key to everything. The financial trap was sprung, not by the girl, but by that other love-hate object, the automobile.

The vehicle I bought, more or less on the spur of the moment, was a maroon 1937 Chevy with four on the floor. Actually, one of those four gears was reverse, and low gear wasn't even syncromeshed. "Syncromesh" was car engineering lingo for manual transmission gears that enabled the driver to shift gears without so much screeching and grating of metal parts. If the transmission had syncromesh gears, one wasn't so likely to hear the taunts of adolescent boys, "They're going to make 'em out of rubber next year!"

In effect, the Chevy had two reasonably useful forward gears. Shifting was accomplished by means of a long, steel rod which came up out of the floor just ahead of the center of the front seat. On the top of the rod was something shaped exactly like a billiard ball, only about half the size. It felt very macho in the palm of the hand.

I had told Ardelle I was getting a new car, a semantic slip made following the excitement of my first large purchase. Needless to say, she was underwhelmed when she saw it. She had been driving a '31 Buick from the farm to school since she was fourteen, and my "new" car wasn't much of an improvement.

"I thought you said the car was new?"

"It's new to me," I apologized. It was a tribute to her character that she did not become my ex-girlfriend on the spot. This was especially true after I asked her for one tiny favor. No, not the money. I had managed a loan from an empathetic banker for the $150 purchase price.

"What do you think could be done with these seats?" I asked shamefully. I had actually been quite proud of my car purchase until that moment. Then I noticed the seats were of questionable construction. Coil springs were protruding through the upholstery on the passenger side. The seats were padded with excelsior and covered with mohair. In case those words are foreign to you, excelsior was a straw-like packing material, while mohair was a closely cropped type of wool upholstery noted for its long wearing capabilities and its bad smell when wet.

The attractive, long legged girl surveyed the car situation, obviously feeling sorry for anyone who would buy such a junkyard escapee. I knew immediately she was going to accept the job. She was taking a class in advanced tailoring, and this was a challenge.

"If you can do something to hold the insides together, I think I can make some seat covers to fit." That's my girl!

My job with bailing wire and a few bolts might strain my mechanical abilities, but her work was not for the faint-hearted. She put in many late night hours sewing those new seat covers. She must love me, I decided. The results, although not spectacular because of the limitations of the original seats, were still by far the best part of the car.

My father had offered his personal expertise in helping me pick out the car. He had a theory. "Chevys are good cars," he said. He had owned two of them, the first being a 1936 model with some sort of short-lived suspension system called "knee action." Round chrome springs stuck out horizontally from the front of the car, inside the open bumper. The result was a ride somewhere between a ten-foot boat on the ocean and a trampoline. Dad's Chevy was the first car I ever drove, and it must have been some sort of weird nostalgia that led me to select a similar one as my first car.

Dad also had owned a 1939 Chevrolet whose principal improvement was that it did not have knee action. That car had a newly rebuilt engine and a shift lever on the steering column. It took strength, plus excellent timing with the clutch pedal, to coax that shifter from one gear to another. Sometimes it simply refused to shift, no matter what the driver did. The cure was to force it into a gear designed to move the car in the opposite direction, which seemed to free up the shift lever. I should have remembered those things before buying my own Chevy.

During World War II, the only new cars being built went to the military. The auto makers had made an amazingly fast conversion to tanks, trucks, and the other heavy machinery of war. Ralph, my father's close friend, was in desperate need of another vehicle. He had purchased a "like new" model from Izzy's Used Car Lot. It had promptly self-destructed. The dealer was entirely unsympathetic when Ralph asked for his money back.

"It run O.K. when you got it," Izzy sneered.

Now fate presented itself. An acquaintance of my father's, a woman whose husband had recently died, had a two-year-old 1940 Buick for sale. She did not know how to drive. Dad bought the big, black Buick Special.

Dad now owned two cars, and nobody needed two cars. The '39 Chevy was only one year older than the Buick, so prospective buyers were everywhere. Ralph needed a car in the worst way. He knew about the rebuilt engine in the Chevy and its bad driving manners. Still, it was only three years old and cars of that age were almost impossible to come by. He made Dad an offer he couldn't refuse.

Dad tried. He pointed out the bad steering and balky gear shift. He told Ralph that he really didn't want to sell the Chevy to a friend, because you just couldn't tell about cars. Ralph bought it anyway.

Strange forces surrounded that Chevy. It had found a home tormenting us. It didn't care for its new housing in Ralph's garage. Therefore, it set itself on fire, burning down Ralph's garage in the process. The fire department decided that it was something in the Chevy's wiring that had started the blaze. Dad and I weren't so sure, knowing the temperment of that vehicle.

Ralph's insurance covered nearly everything, but there was still one minor problem. He couldn't find another car. Ralph was without transportation again. His only choice was to have the burned-out Chevy rebuilt from the ground up.

Temperatures had become so hot during the inferno that the body had been drastically weakened. Therefore, the refurbished car had a skin whose paint was thicker than the metal. The noise inside was deafening at forty miles an hour.

About two years later, just before the war ended, Ralph got a new neighbor. He knew the man: Isadore Cram, the owner of Izzy's Used Car Lot. The same man who had sold Ralph that used car which had expired almost immediately. That disastrous purchase had been the reason Ralph had to borrow the money to buy Dad's '39 Chevy in the first place.

Izzy-the-used-car-salesman was on the lookout for any fairly new car, knowing that he could often double his money overnight. He admired the new paint on Ralph's reconstituted Chevy and approached Ralph about buying it. Ralph was more than ready to sell the noisy vehicle, but not at Izzy's low price. Each week that went by saw a better offer from the used car salesman. The Chevy looked like a high-profit vehicle in Izzy's book.

Finally, Ralph consented to let Izzy drive the car.

"She a bit noisy!" Izzy shouted as they picked up speed. "She ever been wrecked?"

"No. I can personally guarantee this car has never been wrecked," Ralph said, looking him straight in the eye.

"Why she make so damn much racket?"

Ralph shrugged. Izzy bought the car at a much higher figure than he had planned, just days before the Army Air Corps dropped the atomic bomb on Japan that ended the war. New cars weren't available immediately, but people knew they were coming soon and weren't about to buy one of the pre-war models. Izzy had a white elephant. He finally had to keep the car for himself.

Then, like some sort of large, brown snake, the Chevy

began to shed its skin. Finally, it reduced itself to little more than an engine and a crinkled body. Whenever Izzy saw Ralph out in the yard he would ask the same question.

"What'd you do to that damned car?"

"It run O.K. when you got it," Ralph reminded him, as he drove off in the Chrysler he had managed to locate privately.

But I digress. I was telling you about my '37 Chevy with the newly tailored seat covers. It had been given a messy, maroon, "used car" paint job to cover up the rust spots on the body. A new rubber floor mat hid the holes in the floor pan. The car dealer had also used a special black paint on the tire sidewalls. To an inexperienced buyer like me, who didn't look closely at the tread, the tires looked almost new.

Oil pressure was good. I had been told to check the gauge carefully before buying, since low pressure was often a sign of a motor about to die. Only later when some of my mechanically inclined friends took off the valve cover to check out the noise in the rocker arms did we see why the oil pressure was so good. A line had been crimped intentionally with a pair of pliers. No oil could get to the top mechanical parts of the engine, but good oil pressure showed on the gauge. Ah, the trickies!

I'm reminded of the tactics of a friend's older brother. John was an expert at this type of mechanical deception. It would be fair to say that he was living proof that not all of the crooks in the world are selling used cars.

John had a Model A Ford that hadn't run in some time. He needed money to get out of town. Rod bearings were out in the engine and the transmission howled unmercifully between grating noises. John cut some leather strips from worn-out horse harness, oiled them heavily, and inserted them inside the rod bearings. He took a large quantity of fine sawdust and put that in the transmission. Then he hooked up the "A" to a team of horses and pulled it to a bridge just outside a nearby small city. He drove it proudly into the used car lot.

"Got to sell her," he told the dealer. "Farm bills got to be paid. Sure hate to though. She's a real dandy!"

The car salesman was visibly impressed with the quiet running engine and smooth transmission as they drove around the block. He promptly came up with the cash and congratulated himself on a good deal made. Chances are that another trip around the block would have been all the punishment that John's "repair" could have taken before disintegrating. John took the cash and headed for California.

He dreamed up his scams because his habit kept him constantly in need of more money than he could earn legally. He was addicted to very young women. When one ended up pregnant, John either bought his way out of marriage or headed for parts unknown.

Oh . . . about my '37 Chevy. Using it for transportation was a major challenge. In the first place, many of the highways were gravel, not paved. On the frequent fifty-mile trips to see my fiancé, who had taken a teaching job in Loup City, I could count on one or two flat tires or a blowout. With careful planning, two spare tires, a tire pump, a repair kit, and the much-used jack could be sandwiched into the small trunk. This at least raised the odds on getting where I was going.

The cost of tires was a major item in keeping the Chevy mobile. I averaged three new tires per month over the eternity of my indentured ownership. Had I noticed those painted tires when I bought the car I wouldn't have been in quite such a financial hole. Often tires that came with used cars turned the marginal car buyer into a pauper.

The tread on the old bias ply tires squirmed and flexed. As a result, they built up very high levels of heat. This type of construction actually caused them to wear out sooner. Often, it resulted in the sidewalls blowing out from the stress. That meant immediate deflation, and a gaping, non-repairable hole in the sidewall of the offending tire. Since blowouts occurred regularly, the best tires were always put on the rear, or should have been, at least. The theory was that you could

still force steer and make some corrections with a blown-out front tire. If one of the rear tires blew, it was guaranteed to be a wild ride, based solely on just how, and if, the tire and tube stayed on the rim.

What you did not do when you had a blowout was apply the brakes. If you just allowed the car to coast down to a stop it could generally be controlled without too much problem. The natural reaction to a blowout, however, was to jam on the brakes. Usually, this wasn't something you did more than once. A violent uncontrolled skid was a common result.

My tire costs continued to mount. Even new tires wore out in as little as 5,000 miles, since many of the Nebraska roads were still gravel. I was putting about three hundred miles a week on the Chevy, most of it on dates with Ardelle. Most of the money I earned working forty-eight hours a week at a local radio station went to pay my college expenses, car maintenance, car repair, and payments on my car loan. My first hint of financial disaster.

Letters were much too slow to arrange dates, since I usually didn't know if I could get off work until the last minute. Yet tires and other car maintanence expenses had eliminated our long distance phone calls. Ardelle and I devised a code. Every evening at five o'clock I was the announcer of a news and weather program. Ardelle was to listen carefully to my on air remarks for our secret message. If I said, "the temperature right now in downtown Kearney is seventy-eight degrees," it meant I was driving up later that evening.

If I simply said, "the temperature in downtown Kearney is seventy-eight degrees," omitting the "right now," she knew I couldn't make it. My beautiful brunette fiancé made the tiny mistake of letting our little on-air deception out of the bag, thinking that she might be involved in something else and miss my broadcast. Soon, neighbors from all around began calling her. "He's coming up tonight!" Or, "He says he can't make it."

I hadn't considered this as a crafty way to build my listening audience, but it certainly had that effect. On the party phone lines that were common in the rural areas of America then, "rubbering" was a local pastime. This has some similarity to the modern conference call, except with conference calls you know who is on the line. In the old days phone numbers were a series of long and short rings depending on which was assigned as your line. It was wise to listen for the clicks of other receivers being lifted. Some people would simply say, "O.K., is everybody on now so we can go ahead and talk?" This was usually followed by the crashing down of phones by embarrassed listeners, except for the really sneaky ones.

Compounding my tire problems for this long-distance dating was the fact that all tires had inner tubes to hold the air, rather than the tubeless construction used in automobile tires today. Inner tubes had problems even if not punctured. They could slip around inside the tires, pinch, and wear holes in themselves, letting the air escape and causing a flat.

Any self-respecting driver had a tube repair kit in his trunk.

This was a task not usually performed on the side of the road, since it meant removing the inner tube from the tire, scraping an area around the hole in the inner tube with a roughing tool provided in the kit, then applying glue to both the tube and the rubber patch supplied in the kit. The glue was allowed to set up until tacky. The patch and tube were then pressed tightly together until the glue did its job.

Next, the tube was reinserted into the tire and the driver went to work with a hand pump until there was about thirty pounds of air pressure in the tire, or until he lost ten pounds in sweat, which ever came first. That's why repairing tires at the scene of the deflation was avoided whenever possible. There was also the danger that the wrong hole might be patched, or a second one created by stretching the tube where it hadn't quite worn through. That meant starting all over.

Getting to a filling station was the best solution. There was certain to be a tire repair room containing a large, round tank of dirty water. Above the tank was a circular device with metal fingers protruding in all directions. A mechanism would raise and lower this whole contraption. The flat inner tube was over-inflated with air, placed under the metal fingers, and forced down under water.

Then the always grimy tire repairman would exclaim, "There she is! Look at the bubbles!" It was exciting work. He would mark the spot with a piece of white chalk, and then proceed in much the same manner as a driver would with his own patching kit. Most stations had a compressed-air tank to inflate the tube rapidly and then re-submerge it to test the work. It was not unusual for another leak to show up in a different place on a newly repaired tube.

"You got more patches on this than you got tube," was a frequent comment I heard. Or, "Did you know this tire's got a boot in it?" I knew. A "boot" was a large oval piece of rubber, perhaps six to eight inches long, which was bonded to the inside of the tire carcass through a heat process called "vulcanizing." Did you hear that, Mr. Spock? Beam me up,

Scotty!

It was not always a successful process, but vulcanizing sometimes saved the cost of buying another tire when a spike or other sharp object had ripped into the tread portion. Installing a boot properly involved equipment for high temperature heating of the rubber, so it was not a viable alternative for an "at home" fix, although it was often tried.

I soon ran out of money buying new tires for the Chevy and moved into the dangerous area of used tires. These could usually be bought for two or three dollars each, but you could be sure that the previous owner got rid of them for a good reason.

Soon, it seemed, tire changing had become my full time job. I had to find a better alternative. The "recap" seemed to hold the answer. With recaps, the tire tread was removed and a whole new band of tread rubber placed on the casing. This worked, within limits. Still serviceable, worn tire carcasses were basic to the process. Then, if the technician did a good job of "welding" the new rubber tread to the old tire body, it provided a fairly usable tire. Recaps could be bought for about half the cost of new tires, sometimes less.

However, I once hit a pot hole on a road, and heard a huge banging noise that sounded like the entire car was falling apart. A couple hundred yards behind me on the highway lay the entire new tread of my recap in smouldering pieces!

I never really solved my financial problem with tires, even with the lengthy procession of newer cars I bought. The industry eventually took care of the longevity part of it when they developed new, high quality radial tires. Now, if they can just figure out a way to the make money go a little further.

# 2

## *Flummy Diddles*

MANY EXPERIENCES WITH CARS have become part of my family's lore. There was the time Uncle Leonard backed his Ford out of the garage and loaded up his wife and three children for their usual Sunday afternoon drive. A few blocks from the house the car sputtered and came to a halt. His investigation soon found the problem. It was out of gas.

"Why didn't you fill this thing?" He fumed at his wife. "Don't you ever check anything? You should have known it was out of gas!" He continued to berate her.

His wife, Lillian, was a very mild mannered, good natured person, but he had finally crossed the line here.

"You crazy old fool," she said. "You know I can't even drive!"

Uncle Leonard ruled his children with a very firm hand. However, his only daughter, Eva, could wind him around her little finger. Her older brother, Dick, usually got the brunt of Leonard's wrath. In this case, he had severely chastised Dick for some offense, which Dick may or may not have committed.

"Now you shut-up, sit right there in the back seat and tell me if anything's coming," he told his ten year-old son. Leonard proceeded to back out of the narrow, tree-lined drive.

"Still all clear?" he asked.

"Yup," said Dick. More backing.

"Anything coming yet?"

"Nope," said Dick.

C R A S H !!

Leonard jumped out of the car and discovered he had backed into a tree.

"Why in hell didn't you tell me I was going to hit that tree?" he demanded.

"You said tell you if anything was coming, and that tree wasn't," Dick answered, knowing better than to smile.

My Grandmother Plank had driven for many years, but never really mastered the gear shifting on the family Model A Ford. For this reason, I often acted as scout when we went downtown. When grandma approached an intersection that had a stop sign, I looked one way for potentially dangerous vehicles approaching and she looked the other. If it appeared the on-coming cars were moving slowly enough to stop, I would give the all-clear. This way she could avoid stop signs and the resultant gear shifting.

The amazing thing is that I don't believe my grandmother ever was involved in a traffic accident, nor was she ever ticketed for those thousands of stopsign violations.

My wife's German grandmother drove her Chevy coupe primarily around the farm and the six miles into town. I rode with her only once and swore I'd never do it again. Grandma Couton pulled over to the wrong side of the highway whenever she decided she wanted to get a closer look at the neighbor's crops on the left side of the road. "That lazy-ox-

Carpenter didn't get his corn in early enough,'' she sputtered, obviously enjoying the dismal look of her neighbor's stunted crop.

Suddenly a car approached at a high rate of speed and swerved into the other lane just in time to avoid hitting us.

''Hey,'' I shouted in panic, ''that guy almost hit us!'' We continued to cruise on the wrong side of the road near the left ditch.

''Dumb Polack,'' she growled. ''He should know I always drive like this!''

Donald was the son of a highly respected junior high school principal in Grand Island. As with many offspring of pillars of their communities, Donald was a master of the practical joke, particularly when it came to the cars of newly married friends. He appointed himself as chief ''just married'' decorator, can tie-eroner, and mechanical fouler-upper. Donald rarely lacked for assistants, as everyone appreciated his creativity—except the current bride and groom.

His proficiency with wedding getaway cars was very well known among his friends, with each job seeming to surpass the last. He had passed through the smoke bombs and tin cans tied to drive shafts. For the uninitiated, smoke bombs were hooked up to a spark plug wire of the engine. When the vehicle was started it would run very roughly. The wire fastened to the smoke bomb would ignite it through the repeated firings of the engine.

Suddenly, smoke would begin to pour out of the engine compartment, followed by the high-pitched scream of a bomb falling and about to explode. The newlyweds, already harried from the marriage ceremony, would usually panic and leap from the car, at which time the ''bomb'' would make a half-hearted fizzing noise and die out. The fun came from the fact that the wedding guests, who had been tipped off, would then pelt the startled couple with rice for a second time.

As I said, Donald had moved on from these commonplace tricks when our mutual friends Bob and Marge got married.

The couple had purchased a brand-new 1951 Plymouth. Anything was fair game for Donald, but each marriage of his friends required a more elaborate wedding-car stunt. This time he crossed over the line between good fun and foul play.

I freely admit to being a member of the decorating party, but I have always denied participating in the questionable deeds that befell Bob and Marge's new car. However, with white shoe polish in hand, I observed some of the action.

Donald showed up with a pound of Limburger cheese for this newest challenge. He took pieces of that foul smelling, would-be food, and spread it on the exhaust manifold of the new car's engine. His idea was that as soon as the engine warmed up, it would melt the cheese and create an even more rotten odor. He was right.

Not satisfied with this, since the high heat of the manifold was certain to burn off the cheese eventually, Donald filled the heater air intake with more crumbled pieces, and replaced the filter screen on the front so that the cheese wasn't visible. This worked far better than even he had intended.

Whenever the heater was turned on during the winter, the rotten cheese smell permeated the car. Despite repeated efforts over several years, Bob and Marge could never get that rancid, intermittent cheese smell out of the car. Mechanics looked everywhere and never found it. Like most young couples, financial reasons kept them from selling the car for several years. They finally couldn't take the smell any longer and traded it in for another vehicle—during the summer when aroma wasn't brought in through the heater.

When Donald decided to marry, he was well aware that his car would be the target of almost everyone whose wedding he had ever attended. Immediately following the ceremony, the bride and groom ran outside through the usual hail of rice. Then they led the procession back into the church to begin the reception line.

However, in all the typical wedding reception confusion, Donald and his new bride slipped out the back door. In seconds this was noticed by the car-decorating crowd and they headed for the same exit. To their surprise, they found the door securely locked from the outside. They dashed to the front of the church, but Donald had beaten them there as well. He left the key he had stolen in the outside lock. The entire wedding party and guests were all locked inside the church, while Donald casually drove away in a perfectly normal car.

The Limburger cheese in the earlier episode brings to mind one of my father's most notable projects. Dad was an ardent catfish fisherman. He and his friends, Jasper and Abe, experimented endlessly in an attempt to find the very finest catfish bait in the world.

They used chicken entrails, chicken entrails left in the sun for several days, or chicken entrails stripped out and soaked in buttermilk and cornmeal. Their theory was often repeated that the three dirtiest eaters in the world were chickens, hogs, and catfish, not necessarily in that order.

They used dried chicken blood, sometimes coagulated on small pieces of sponge, chicken livers, or sliced up internal parts of various animals. They used mice, frogs, decomposing small fish, strong cheeses, and just about anything that was "ripe." (Are you sick yet?) Catfish fishermen from all walks of life still use these concoctions, yet nothing could be found that would "stay on the hook," or give off a long-lasting aroma and still catch fish when the water was muddy.

The three put their heads together and through trial and error came up with a superior catfish bait. It was composed of thin sliced pieces of something they called "hog melts," a non-edible, toughened internal organ of the hog. They added Limburger cheese and cod liver oil.

Then came the magic ingredient, ambergris. For those readers who are not into zoology, ambergris is a grayish, waxy substance secreted from the intestines of sperm whales. It is found floating in tropical seas in huge chunks ranging up to

200 pounds. Ambergris has an extremely strong odor. So strong that it has been used for years in the making of quality perfumes with a lingering scent.

Just who among the three catfishermen came up with the idea of using ambergris in catfish bait is unknown to me. I doubt that any of them did. Like most of us, they had probably never heard of the stuff. They ordered the material through the Rexall Drugstore, which leads me to suspect that they had an outside adviser who came up with this odoriferous ingredient.

In watching the making of the bait, I remember that only a small piece of ambergris was placed in the mix. When it was melted in the cooking process, it turned a yellowish color and added a powerful scent to the already aromatic concoction.

The first bait-cooking experiment occurred in our basement over a camp stove. The strange thing is that while it was brewing, everyone was oblivious to the gradually worsening smell. Perhaps it was the anticipation of a revolutionary new fish bait, or perhaps it was like boiling a frog. You can take a live frog and put him in boiling water and he will immediately leap out to safety. Take that same frog, put him in a pot of cool water on the stove and gradually heat it. The frog will be cooked in it without any reaction on his part. (I've never tried this, but that's what I'm told.)

My mother was out playing bridge that evening, but we all knew the minute she got home. The fishermen and the new bait were banished from the premises forever and ever. Still anxious to try this promising catfish bait, Dad and his co-conspirators drove up to the Loup River that same night and in a very short time had a huge number of unusually aggressive catfish.

"They went crazy over that stink bait," Dad told me. Mom finally let Dad come back home after his solemn promise to never again cook stink bait in or near our house.

Now plans had to be laid to find a location for cooking up

a new batch. House by house, they were evicted by the screams of wives—"What's that horrible smell?" But catfishermen are a determined lot, especially when the fishing results were so amazing.

Finally they made a deal with Harv Stahlnecker, up on the north edge of town, to use an old, unused outhouse far back at the rear of his property for cooking the bait. They covered the outhouse holes with a wide board and cooking continued. They provided Harv with a supply of stink bait in payment for the use of the facility. Harv was a dedicated catfisherman himself, and this new bait enhanced his reputation. Soon questions were being asked about this magic bait and it became something of a phenomenon.

A local dentist was an ardent catfisherman and asked to buy some of the product. The guys figured that it was only fair to charge something, since they had the cost of materials and their time involved. So their first commercial deal was struck. A quart jar full of stink bait for seventy-five cents.

Soon they were having trouble keeping up with demand.

They decided to go into real production. Each had his own job. Jasper lined up the new quart cans and a lid-sealing machine. They ordered labels printed with pictures of catfish. Abe found the larger production quarters they needed and the building was rented. Dad was busy taking orders and selling the product. Their choice of names for the bait was H.T.R. after the initials in each last name, Hodges, Thompson, and Rice. If I had been old enough to have a vote I think I would have suggested the highly descriptive "stink bait" as a name.

Investments were made in new cooking units and large-scale quantities of the ingredients. Distribution began to a number of retail outlets. H.T.R., the miracle catfish bait, was selling out of control. Expansion plans were evolved as the wealth of the three entrepreneurs seemed assured. There was talk of quitting day jobs to keep up with production demand. Fortunately, before that happened, other events came about.

The first hint of trouble came from their dentist customer. His catfishing was confined to Saturday evenings, he explained, and it was several weeks before he had a chance to try out the bait. When he returned to work Monday morning, having thoroughly washed his hands many times, there was no trace of smell from H.T.R. His first case was a particularly tough extraction on a woman patient. It was warm in the office and he began to perspire. Suddenly it was there. The unmistakable stink bait smell.

He excused himself and washed his hands with a strong soap and returned to his dental work. There it was again, wafting up from his hands near the lady's nose. Finally he had to re-schedule her. She apparently decided the toothache was better than the smell and cancelled altogether. Doc tried everything he could think of and even washed his hands in gasoline, before giving up his practice for the day.

"I tried wearing rubber gloves to put that stuff on the hook, and even then my hands got full of that stink," he said. The dentist was no longer a customer for H.T.R. bait because of professional considerations.

About that same time, Dad left a half-open can of H.T.R in the trunk of his 1929 Pontiac following a fishing trip. He promptly forgot about it after cleaning a huge stringer of catfish. The Pontiac had a box-like trunk that was detached from the car itself.

As the summer temperature reached ninety degrees, everybody in the neighborhood, including Dad, was out looking for the animal that had died. They searched under enclosed porches, garages, and took apart wooden lattice work. Finally someone with a direction-oriented nose pinpointed the Pontiac trunk. When it was opened, a green gas of fumes nearly blinded bystanders. We were not the most popular family on the block, even after Dad took the can out in the country and buried it.

Then came the real trouble for the catfish bait enterprise. A grocer in Palmer owned a store on the east side of Main Street. He had purchased a large quantity of H.T.R. and decided to make a pyramid window display of the amazing bait.

As the summer sun worked its way around to shine on the plate glass, temperatures soared in the display window. There was an afternoon lull in business and the grocer and his wife were in the office at the rear of the store making out orders. Suddenly there was a loud bang.

"What the hell was that?" the grocer asked.

Before his wife could answer, there was another explosion, followed by poofing noises. The couple ran out into the main store just as a woman entered. Stink bait covered the window. Stink bait covered the ceiling. Stink bait was dripping down onto the fresh fruits and vegetables. The lady pulled a handkerchief from her purse, gagged, and retreated out the door. A nightmare of brown-green stench that even Stephen Spielberg might have trouble imagining was erupting in the grocery display window.

The irate grocer and the H.T.R. group discovered that

heating the cans caused the bait to expand drastically and ultimately to explode. There were hurried trips to businesses all around the area as the trio refunded money and took back hundreds of quart cans before more disasters could occur.

We still used the legendary H.T.R. to catch catfish for some time. Each partner took one-third of the cans and kept them in cool storage. As far as I know, nobody ever had nerve enough to cook up another batch of stink bait. It's probably just as well, or there might not be any catfish left in the rivers.

# 3

# *Caveats and Cadillacs*

AFTER CONSIDERING THE FINANCIAL PROBLEMS associated with catfish bait production, I'm reminded of that other stinker, my '37 Chevy. The Chevy had an engine with low-tech engineering, even for the 1930s models. It used an "oil bath" system for lubricating the heavy-duty parts enclosed in the lower engine pan.

Engine bearings were lubricated by a "splash" method whereby the commotion in that lower area of the engine was supposed to keep things oiled. At best it did so unevenly, often resulting in the deadly "clunk, clunk" disease.

The clunk, clunk disease heralded the later "Slam! Bang! Crash! Stop!" disorder. This was very costly. The engine on the old Chevy was easier to overhaul than most because it used a material called babbitt in the rod bearings. A rod is a thingamajig fastened at the bottom to the crank-shaft and at the top to the piston. The number of pistons in a car tells you if you have a four-, six- or eight-cylinder engine. Of course, you can't see the pistons, so you just have to take the carmaker's word for it.

Precision fitting of bearing surfaces had always been difficult for engine manufacturers, particularly the rod bearings. Chevy found a way to ignore this problem by using babbitt in the engine bearings. This is a very soft metal that wears away until the bearings fit, hence the renowned "break-in" period for Chevy engines. They were easier for a backyard, do-it-yourself mechanic to work on, however.

Once the engine was "broken in," it was all downhill as far as precision fit was concerned. Bearings kept wearing away eventually causing the dreaded clunk, clunk disease. You might think such engineering genius would be short-lived. However, babbitt stayed around in some Chevrolet engines until the early 1950s.

Writer Sinclair Lewis even named a novel *Babbitt* after the book's principal character. Naturally, he didn't wear well either.

I knew virtually nothing about cars when I bought my '37 Chevy. If I had, I would have found something in better repair. Today there are publications, including *Consumer Reports*, that evaluate everything from the safety of specific models to just which vehicles are likely to be the most trouble-free as used cars. If you want to spend a little research time, you won't be at the mercy of the seller today as a buyer was in years past.

New-car advertising has a direct effect on used-car buyers since the advertised features usually stay around for several years. It is fortunate that the slick ad writers didn't have one of our local businessmen working for them.

Armand and his staff did high quality upholstery work for both the home and car. He also had an idea for a new product for which he saw a high demand here in the Bible belt. It was a good idea. Armand designed a portable church pew that was fully upholstered and padded, so that those attending services in new buildings would not be placed in the predicament of the mind only being able to absorb what the rear could endure. These portable seats could easily be rearranged at any time and offered multiple uses for the sometimes financially strapped congregations.

Armand's problem came in that he wanted full control, without professional advice, in the naming of his new product, and in how it was advertised. I'll never forget the first time I saw the beautiful four-color brochure he had printed to promote his product. Right at the top in huge letters was the name of the portable church furniture:

**Armand's Instant Pew**

Certainly this would have been an appropriate name for my Dad's ill-fated catfish bait. Armand's spelling was correct, but when the ads hit radio and TV, the result was not what he wanted.

Automobile advertising sales pitches usually extol some of the most ridiculous gimmicks ever to come out of Detroit. For instance, ad men justified tail fins on cars in the 1950s by explaining that they kept the car from "fish tailing" at high speeds. This was engineering by public relations departments. If the fins had any effect on a car, it would have to be at speeds far in excess of the top miles-per-hour even the biggest engine could reach.

Then, in the same decade another styling excess was born. Wraparound windshields were called a safety design because there was a straight post from the roof, rather than the slanted ones we are accustomed to. Much better visibility was the reason given for the change. Problems? Not if you didn't mind banging your knees on the windshield pillar that intruded one-third of the way into the normal door opening. Looking through that sharply curved corner of the glass provided a view so distorted it was reminiscent of the old carnival Fun House mirrors.

The least expected result of the straight-pillar windshield

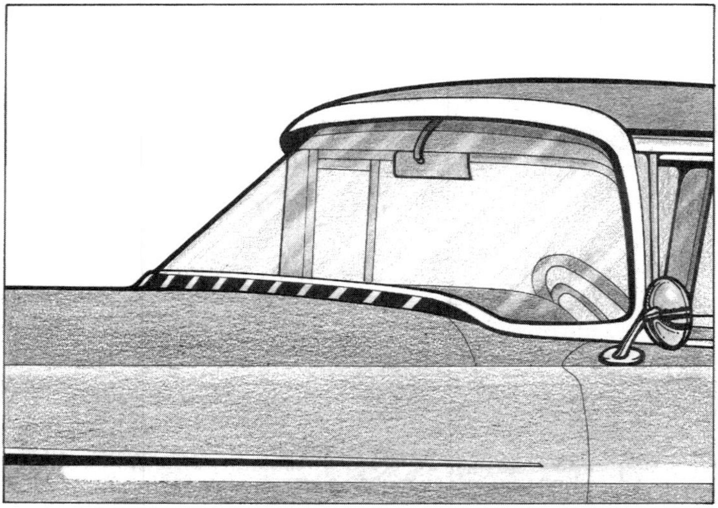

was that it hid narrow vertical objects from the driver's view in a blindspot. Nothing important. Just vertical objects like people, bicycles, motorcycles, telephone poles . . . things like that. With a standard, diagonal windshield post you could at least see enough of these objects to know there was something there that you didn't want to hit. Reason eventually prevailed and wraparound windshields are now seen as a curiosity on a few automobile collectibles.

Fully enclosed rear tires were another idea nobody thought through before building. Cadillac, and many other cars, had removeable trim plates at the rear that made changing tires a time-consuming job. The wheel-opening covers looked streamlined, but since even prestige cars were plagued by frequent flats, they were a pain, particularly in bad weather.

Nash motors carried this even further and enclosed the front wheels without access panels. It is likely that the first vehicle to use this "streamlining" was a show car designed by Chrysler in 1941 called the Thunderbolt. This car had a tiny bubble cockpit with about eight feet of hood in front of it and eight feet of trunk to the rear. The Thunderbolt never reached production. It was totally impractical, of course, but in 1949 Nash Motors picked up the enclosed front wheel design from that one-of-a-kind styling experiment.

The idea was ninety-eight percent styling, explained by the advertised notion that it cut down on wind drag. It also gave the car a turning radius about the same as a Boeing 747. These designs, called by many people "upside-down-bathtubs," disappeared in about three years, perhaps because no one could change those enclosed front tires.

A true engineering innovation in the automobile industry was introduced by Chrysler Motors in the 1930s with its "Airflow" design. The Chrysler and DeSoto unit bodies, with all welded construction, were incorporated into one of the first mass production attempts at aerodynamic design. It was far too advanced for the car buying public. Unlike today, most buyers of that time did not believe that newer was necessarily better. In any event, the Airflow design nearly bankrupted Chrysler. The company was forced to return to old technology.

Nash and Hudson Motors reintroduced the concept in the late 1940s. Nash began its post-war production with all welded construction in 1947, but retained a styling much like the pre-World War II cars, until the major jelly-bean shape change in 1949.

Hudson's 1948 "step down" design was ridiculed by rival car salesmen and manufacturers. The Hudson design had a sill at each door while the entire inside floor was lowered about four inches.

"How do they expect you to sweep out the floor of the car over that sill?" non-Hudson salesmen would ask. "That's got to be the dumbest thing anybody ever built. Do away with the flat floor? Never!" People didn't have to vacuum their car floors prior to the "step down" design.

The flat-floor people would have been flat-earth people, had they lived in Columbus's time. Hudson proved its low center of gravity design on the race track, winning nearly all of the events it entered. Although Hudsons were an excellent design

and gained some converts, they were generally a failure in the marketplace.

Being ahead of current design, even in those rare instances when a truly superior innovation in an automobile happened, was extremely risky to the manufacturer. The value of unit body, or all-welded construction, with step-down passenger compartment is clear today. Almost all cars are built using very similar designs.

Nash's "weather eye" heating and ventilation system was years ahead of its time. It worked by pulling outside air in through a wide vent at the base of the windshield, instead of through a small opening near the grill.

Reclining seats were also a Nash innovation. Even before World War II, in the late 1930s, the company introduced "the seats that make into a bed." A local radio announcer ad libbed commercials for a Nash dealer and always referred to the cars as "perambulating boudoirs." Loosely translated, this meant "beds that walk around," and attributed certain sexual connotations to the car.

Nash had another interesting feature. A pod containing all the instruments and the speedometer was mounted on the steering column, just behind the wheel. It was called a "Uniscope." The instrument cluster was very difficult to work on, and its reliability was not good. If modern electronic instruments and micro-circuits had been invented at the time, we might still have the Uniscope display. A quick glance at the gauges told you everything. Since it was higher up, and

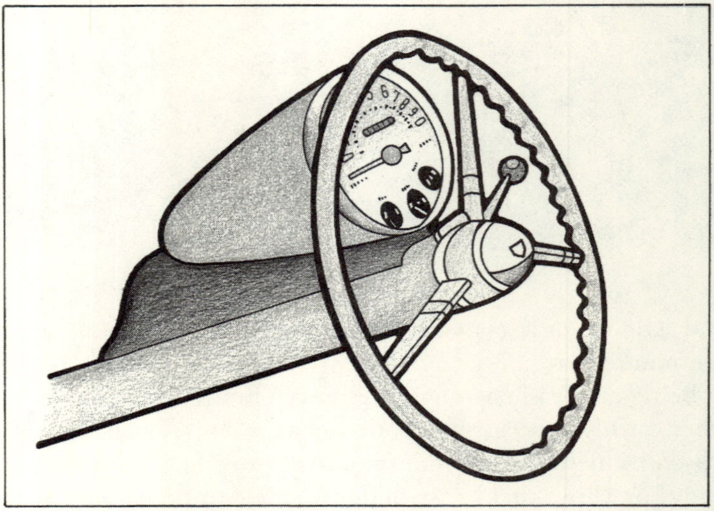

closer to the driver, the eyes barely left the road. There are probably safety implications in that location since the advent of collapsible steering columns or the Uniscope might have been revived.

Fake spare tires, the last vestiges of ''continental kits,'' began in the 1950s to replace actual external mounted spare tires. The styling remnants have been carried through, primarily on the Lincoln Mark series. On the 1992 models there is little more than a small bump in the trunk lid to suggest what was once the tire. This has about the same relationship to a wheel as our human tailbone has to a tail.

The pseudo spare tires are certainly a lot better than the real ones that were mounted on the exterior of the trunk. If you had a flat tire, it was a major job just to get the tire removed from its ornate metal case.

Furthermore, drivers had to put up with that lousy tire location for the sake of styling in day-to-day use. The spare was just big enough to block putting large objects into the trunk on either side of it. Going up over the spare with anything larger than a cosmetic case was next to impossible. Some spare

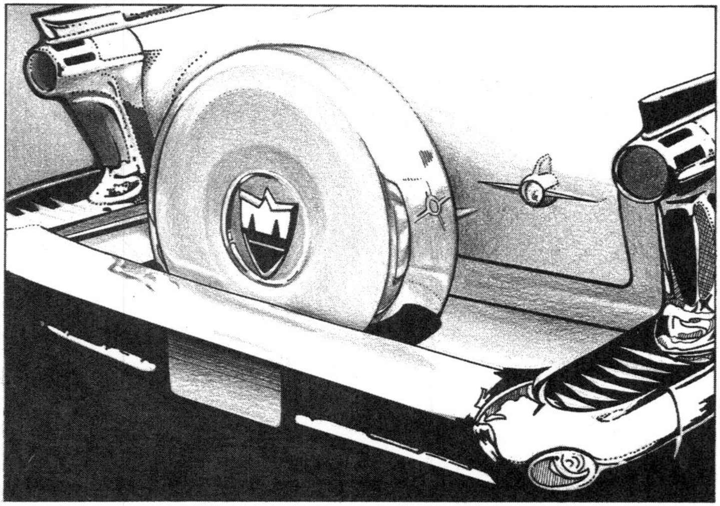

tire cases folded down away from the rear bumper. This helped some, but you still had to figure out how to manage that enormous reach over the spare laid horizontally behind the trunk. Often the only solution was to lift the luggage over the side of the rear fender which proved to be an excellent way to bang your head on the open trunk lid.

Buicks of the 1950s had fake exhaust-ports in the front fenders reminiscent of the classic Cord automobile minus its chrome exhaust tubes. These chrome holes in the side of Buick's front fenders were status symbols; the more holes, the more expensive the car. (Do you suppose that some of today's blue-jean companies got their sales philosophy from Buick?) A number of cars had artificial air scoops raised into the hood, a styling trick stolen from hot rodders who used functional, open scoops to drive more air into their carburetors. The simulated scoop was meant to suggest speed and power, like the muscle cars of the 1950s and 1960s.

Cars with push-button automatic transmission controls were another engineering innovation gone awry. Some Chrysler products had them on the left side of the dash. The Edsel carried this a step further and put the buttons in the center of the steering wheel. Ford Motor Company would just as soon forget about that: both the transmission buttons and the Edsel.

For sheer functional waste, look at the radios on some present-day General Motors cars. The sound system has so many small controls and tiny buttons on it that it is almost impossible to operate it while driving. Rather than correct this, GM put duplicate radio controls in the center of the steering wheel on some upscale models. A few auto enthusiasts actually trumpeted this as a great engineering accomplishment! It seems they never considered the large extra costs involved in duplicate radio controls, let alone the complexities. The simple fix of larger, fewer, easier-to-operate controls on the radio itself would have been the real engineering acomplishment. In any event, air bags in the steering wheel will eliminate that excess.

Recently Ford attempted to transfer European ergonomics to America by placing the horn in a button at the end of the turn signal stalk. Nobody ever found that. People thought the car just had a horn that didn't work and almost broke the palms of their hands pounding the hub of the steering wheel trying to make it honk.

Then there were vinyl-roofed cars. For nearly a twenty-year period spanning the mid 1960s to the 1980s, the vinyl roof was pervasive in all American prestige lines. This was baffling to me until I learned the secret.

I have test-driven many vehicles with padded roofs, so I know this is true even though I've never owned one. If a car has a vinyl roof, it is quite likely to drive like a water bed.

I'm not exactly sure why there is a direct relationship between vinyl roofs and sloppy handling. All I know is that there seems to be one. Obviously, it is also possible to have bad road manners in a car without a vinyl roof: it's just not quite as likely.

The vinyl roof is just another prestige fad that has about

run its course. Many vinyl roofs today are rotting off the older models as city air pollution or acid rain goes to work on them. Strangely, a case can even be made linking the decline of the American car market directly to the introduction of the vinyl roof!

There is something magical about the name Cadillac, especially among older Americans who associate the name with the ultimate in quality. "It's the Cadillac of vacuum cleaners," a salesman will say, meaning it's the best. There is naturally controversy surrounding this appraisal, especially from Lincoln and certain foreign car manufacturers.

Bill worked as an accountant at our local Cadillac agency. He was a jazz aficionado and moonlighted in a local combo. For background purposes, you should be aware that Bill tipped a few on a regular basis. His favorite line to liven up parties was a hearty, "I feel more like I do now than I did when I came in."

This line usually left guests in an amused, if somewhat bewildered, state. If it made sense to anyone, they'd had one too many "sodie pops," as Bill called anything with ice cubes in it.

Although employed in a Cadillac agency, it would be fair to say that Bill did not like cars, and in particular he didn't like Cadillacs. Some of his life's worst experiences seemed to involve Cadillacs.

"Man, every time I get close to one of those things some sort of disaster happens," he said, "Never figured out if its the cars or the dudes that drive 'em."

When Bill retired, he looked for a warmer climate, settling in sunny New Mexico. He was never a sit-still kind of person. That's how he got hooked up with "Digger." Digger was the local mortician, appropriately nicknamed. As their friendship grew, Digger offered Bill a job as an assistant mortician. Reluctant at first, Bill's offbeat sense of humor served him well.

"Corpses are just like so much cord wood once you start

workin' with 'em,'' he remarked. Soon Bill and Digger agreed that Bill just didn't have the proper touch for women's makeup and hair styles. Bill's wife Ava soon joined the firm and took over those chores.

Bill's constant string of funeral jokes relegated him to ''inside man at the skunk works,'' as he referred to his part of the job. Digger, wisely, was afraid to turn Bill loose with the mourners, until one day he found himself in a real bind. Two of his full-time employees got sick on the same day, and it happened to be the day of not one, but two funerals of the town's dignitaries.

''You ever drove a hearse?'' Digger asked skeptically.

''Man, you askin' some cat who worked thirty years for a Cadillac dealer whether he ever drove a hearse? That's all they make!''

This seemed to satisfy Digger. ''Let's get serious here,'' he said nervously. ''Since we've only got the one hearse, and it could be dusty on the road to the cemetery, we've got a bit of a logistics problem. There won't be time to wash it in between ceremonies, so suppose you just give it a funeral wash.''

''A what?''

''A funeral wash. That's where you dust off the trim, polish the bumpers and wash the white wall tires. Take you about five minutes and nobody'll know the difference,'' Digger said impatiently.

''Well ain't that sumpthin','' Bill said, ''Ain't even got time to give 'em their last ride in a clean hearse.''

Digger ignored the remark. ''You know the way to the cemetery?'' he asked.

''Yeh, but I ain't in no hurry to get there.'' There was more truth to that than Bill realized.

''I'll draw you a map of the exact route you take from the church. It's up there in a kind of ritzy neighborhood with streets laid out every which way. You won't have any trouble if you just follow the street signs.''

"Where you gonna be? Putting in a word with the Almighty?"

"I've got that other service right after this one," Digger replied. "You're going to have to line up the pallbearers, drive the hearse, and lead the procession."

Digger was still skeptical about putting Bill in charge, especially when he saw some 200 cars lined up in the funeral procession.

"Tell you what," Digger said, "why don't you take Ava along with you and she can make sure there aren't any direction problems. That's really a bunch of cars. I'd just as soon pay for her time and ease my mind a bit—not that I don't think you can handle it," he added hastily.

They hit upon a sure-fire plan of attack. Ava was to stand on the sidewalk about two blocks from the church where the first tricky corner occurred and signal the correct turn for Bill and the hearse containing the recently departed.

Bill had been on his best behavior during the actual funeral service and was congratulating himself on his excellent deportment. He drove off slowly in the long, black Cadillac hearse. Two hundred cars followed faithfully through the crooked streets when suddenly Bill discovered to his horror that he was lost. Not just lost, but he had driven into a cul de sac.

He made the circle and proceeded out on the same street he had entered as the long procession of cars dutifully followed.

"I had to drive right back by every one of those damned cars with all of those cowboys staring at me like I was crazy," he said. "First street I came to that looked halfway familiar I let her rip and headed for the tombstones. Fastest funeral procession those dudes were ever in!"

Digger was appropriately horrified when he heard about the fiasco.

"Why didn't you turn him in the right direction like I showed you on the map?" he demanded of Ava.

"I did everything but stand on my head," she retorted. "I was waving my arms, pointing and yelling, and that dingbat just turned around the corner the other way!''

I've often wondered what the people living at the end of the cul de sac must have thought.

''Hey, Mom, come quick. I think we got a whole bunch of company!''

Back in the rural areas of Nebraska, ''company'' was something most farm families looked forward to. This was in the days before good rural roads and reliable automobiles. Everyone was an honored guest. Chances were a complete stranger would be invited to spend the night, share a meal, or at least have lunch. To some extent the tradition continues to this day.

My friend Eddie advised me that not quite everyone was welcome. In his best imitation of an event which apparently had often taken place in his farm home as a youngster, Eddie would say, ''Quick, Ma! Hide the younguns and get back from the windas! It's them danged surveyors again!''

Evidently that had something to do with roads, railroads, power or telephone line taking part of the farmstead land. It could also have been arguments with neighbors over fence lines, dams or drainage locations, or anything that involved some outsider ''surveyin' the property.''

I mention this for two reasons. Ed was an insurance agent. Insurance people are not always much more welcome guests among farmers than the surveyors were, although Eddie certainly was. Secondly, Eddie was as much a Cadillac fan as Bill, the mortician-cum-travel-agent, hated them.

Ed drove a twenty-foot-long, tail-finned behemoth. ''From the moment I saw the 1949 Cadillac I knew it was the car for me,'' he said. ''I saved my money until I had enough to buy that '49. Of course, it was 1960 by then.''

This cost business is always relative, but in the early 1990s there are fifty-four different makes of cars sold in the U.S. priced at more than $30,000, and ranging upwards to the $215,000 for a top-level Rolls Royce. Some exotic sports cars have even higher price tags. We have now reached a level where we no longer necessarily express the cost of a new car as a percentage of the cost of a house. For instance my '53 Plymouth equalled about twenty percent of the cost of our first house. Nonetheless, we still haven't reached the point where a buyer's rule of thumb should be, "Never buy a car that costs more than your house." Real estate generally appreciates over a few years, while automobiles depreciate.

A current 300E class Mercedes Benz retains about fifty percent of it's original cost after four years. That is the least depreciation of any sedan sold in America. Some high-level sports cars, and certain classics or antiques retain more value. The reason this car leads in resale value is its perceived quality and excellent repair record.

Can we draw any financial conclusions from this? Perhaps. For example, the top-of-line 500 SL Mercedes lists for some $84,500, but doesn't fare quite so well over four years in the depreciation department. According to the National Automobile Dealer Association current average retail price, the four-year-old car still has a respectable value of about $41,000, or nearly fifty percent of original cost. Now let's compare those dollar results to an American-made Cadillac.

Suppose you bought a top-line Cadillac Fleetwood for about $32,500 in 1992 dollars. After the same four-year period, it would be worth only about thirty-four percent of its purchase price. However, there's more to the equation. The actual dollar loss on the Cadillac would be about $21,400, or only a tad over half the dollar loss on the Mercedes. I'll leave it to you to determine which is the better buy. If you think the Mercedes is at least twice as good as the Cadillac you'll do well to purchase that vehicle. On the other hand you could buy two Fleetwoods, store one in the garage for future use or a chance for premium resale.

Eddie, the vintage Cadillac driver, always had tricks up his sleeve to cope with the unexpected. He drove his Cadillac in his work, even in the rural area. I was riding with him on one such appointment when he drove into a farmyard. We were greeted by a ferocious German shepherd. The dog jumped at the car, his toenails screeching down the highly polished paint. Then he bit at the window trim, snarling all the time.

Ed was incensed that the dog was mangling his pride and joy, but he certainly wasn't foolish enough to get out of the car with this monster guarding the farmyard. Ed used the time-honored signal to the farmer to call off the dog, honking the horn. No one was home. Ed pulled out of the yard as the barking shepherd ripped at the tires.

When we were safely down the road, Ed stopped the car. First he surveyed the damage done to the paint and trim. "Damn dog," he muttered. Then he opened the trunk and took out a loose woven gunny sack. He took off the huge left front hubcap of the Caddy, put the gunny sack under it, and pounded the hub cap back on.

"What in thunder are you doing?" I asked.

"Gonna teach that dog some manners," he replied. Slowly, he drove back to the farm driveway. At once the dog spotted the car and attacked the whirling cloth on the front wheel. Just as he sunk his teeth into it, Ed hit the accelerator. The dog sailed into the air higher than the hood and landed with a startled crash in a nearby plum thicket.

"Bet when I come back to see these folks that ornery critter's gonna be just as nice as you please to my car!" crowed Ed.

Several years ago three couples from different small Nebraska towns planned to attend a regional business conference in Florida. We decided it might be fun to travel together, providing we had a large enough vehicle.

Meyer volunteered. "Let's drive up in a Cadillac limousine! That'll show all them eastern dudes a thing or two." The more we discussed this premise, the implications of arriving in a limo from out here in the sticks, the better it began to sound.

". . . And red Cornhusker jackets, with big red cowboy hats," I chimed in. "And all of us shoutin' 'Go Big Red'!"

Kay, the most socially conscious of the group and one who had never been to one of these conventions, decided it was definitely the thing to do.

"That sounds like a very sound idea to me," she told Meyer. "You'll arrange for the limousine then?" Kay looked at him primly.

None of us had the heart to tell her that this sort of inane banter went on all the time, that no one had any intention of really doing it.

Meyer looked at me. I looked at the floor. This was Meyer's move and he knew it.

"Well, maybe we ought to, uh, think about this a little bit. It could cost quite a bit—" He trailed off. It may have just hit him for the first time that this woman was not going to let him off the hook.

"There are three couples," Kay said. "We can divide the rental costs and the gasoline three ways. That way we'll be able to take along all the clothes we want."

The other two women, although knowing what was going on, nodded in enthusiastic agreement.

"Sure, Meyer," I said, "Why don't you just get a limo from the Cadillac dealer in Hastings. I understand he's got one he rents for parties and college social events."

Meyer was beginning to wish he had never brought up the subject, as he really wasn't in the position to spend the kind of money it might take to pull off this caper. "O.K., I'll check into it," he said with an air of resignation, knowing he had been trapped.

A few days later, Meyer called and said, "I've got the Cadillac."

"You do?" I said suspiciously, since I knew Meyer's wild-eyed ideas quite well.

"Yup. We'll pick you and Ardelle up first and then on to Morris and Kay's."

I couldn't believe he had actually done it. Then a thought crept in. "Just how much is this rental going to cost us for two weeks, Meyer?"

"A hundred and fifty bucks apiece," he said jubilantly.

"My gosh, that's only $450 for two weeks." Even in those inflationless days of the early 1960s, that was a real bargain. "How did you manage to swing it?"

"You always smirk when I tell you about my connections. This time the laugh's on you," he gloated.

In the early morning darkness of the day we were scheduled to leave, a large car rolled up into our driveway. It was a big, black, four-door Cadillac all right, but certainly not a limo, and certainly not new.

"What's this thing?" I asked suspiciously. "Where's the limo?"

"The limos got booked up at the last minute for a couple of parties this week, so I did the next best thing and got this one," Meyer responded. I doubted there had ever been a limo deal, but I kept quiet.

"We can't get all that stuff the women are bringing into the trunk of that old beater," I observed. "Did you try to get a luggage rack for the top?"

"No way. We're not gonna pull up there to that posh hotel lookin' like a band of traveling gypsies. No, sir. Everybody gets one suitcase and an overnight case, and that's it." Meyer was adamant.

After a hurried phone call to Morris and Kay advising them of the situation, we began repacking and eliminating some of our bags. After we put our luggage in the trunk, we could see it was going to be a very tight fit at the next stop.

When we arrived at Morris and Kay's, they greeted us at the door with the correct number of bags, but Kay's was about the size of the average steamer trunk.

We unloaded everything. We put the huge case in and tried repacking. Not even close.

"All right, Kay, you've got to pack that into a normal size

suitcase," Meyer said.

She became irate. "I will not leave anything else at home. I've already had to leave out four good dresses and six pairs of shoes." She stared defiantly at Meyer. "You said this was going to be a limo, and it's just an old car. I will not leave out anything more!"

I could see our group of happy campers, riding six in a car for 4,500 miles wasn't getting off on the right foot.

"Hold it," I said. "I've got an idea that just might let us get it all in." I loosened the large spare tire from its housing, took it out and threw it on the floor of Morris's garage. With a great deal of pushing and wedging, we managed to get all the luggage in and crammed down the trunk lid.

"Only a bunch of fools would try to drive 4,500 miles without a spare tire," Meyer, a one-time truck driver, observed. He was certainly right. It was nearly impossible to drive that far, even over good paved highways, without getting a flat or blowout, even with new tires.

"What are the alternatives?" I asked.

Meyer knew, but he didn't figure he could tell Morris and Kay to drive their own car, especially not in light of the fact this Cadillac "limo" has been his idea.

I took Meyer aside. "How are the tires on this thing?"

"Not the greatest," he said, "and the springs are about down on the axle now the way we're loaded."

My fears were unfounded. We made it all the way to Miami without tire trouble and with friendships intact. Meyer had even gotten the red jackets and cowboy hats for our grand entrance at the Fontainbleau. With all of us men at over six feet we became instantly recognizable as Nebraskans. My wife thought we looked like a bunch of giant sky caps trying out for the rodeo.

The conference was memorable. At one point Meyer, red jacket, big mouth, and all, ended up in a swimming pool. The chlorine turned the red wool jacket a sickly pink. Once we heard the splash and saw that red jacket in the pool, we all quietly left the poolside dinner and changed clothes while Meyer's wife locked herself in the bathroom.

The ride home was harrowing. We ran into frequent highway construction, and three days with six people in one car (some of whom still weren't speaking to each other) was three days too long, no matter how big the car was. I was driving in a pouring rain somewhere in Arkansas when suddenly the rear end let down with a noisy thud. We had blown a tire.

"OK," everybody said at once, "whose bright idea was it to leave the spare at home?" I knew. "The driver is the one who has to get out in this rain and go get help." It was almost a unanimous vote.

After a wet hike of several hundred yards, I walked up a very long drive to a huge house and rang the doorbell. A man answered. I explained the situation.

"Ya'll drove all the way from where? Did you say, Nebraska, with no spare tire on that Caddy? Man, ya'll must be plumb crazy!" He laughed at the thought of it.

"Wal, ole son, ya'll just may be in luck. Happens that both my wife and I drive Cadillacs. I won't drive a set of tires more'n 8,000 miles before I put a new set on both cars. Always keep the old uns though, cause they don't give you nothin' for a trade in no more. Use 'em on the farm trailers now and again."

He took me out to a huge garage, and just as he had said, there were neatly stacked piles of tires, all of them in better shape than any we were driving on.

"Ya'll just take your pick. You got a jack with you?"

"No." That was back home in Morris's garage too.

"Haw!" He was still savoring this. "We're just fixin' to leave, but I'm gonna call the station and have the tire man get up here right away and he can put it on the rim for you. Haw! All the way from Nebraska with no spare." He shook his head in disbelief.

"I can't tell you how much we appreciate this," I told him.

"I don't know what we would have done—"

"Ya'll woulda done the same thing for me if I was in such a dumb fool spot, wouldn't ya?"

"I sure would, sir, only I don't have a garage full of Cadillac tires," I admitted. "What do we owe you for the tire and the service call?" The service truck was driving up the lane now.

"Not a thing. Hell, no. Ya'll just remember that when somebody breaks down and needs some help, especially if they're Razorbacks!" He guffawed.

"Thanks a lot," I said. "You have no idea what it means to have at least one good tire on that car!"

Very soon we were on our way again. "Well, how much is it going to cost each of us?" Meyer asked from his dry shelter in the back seat.

"Fifty bucks each," I said solemnly to a series of groans, before telling them the truth.

"Well, I'll be damned," Morris-the-Sunday-school-teacher intoned excitedly.

"Double damned," said Meyer. "That's the luckiest thing I ever heard of in my whole life. In the middle of a rainstorm, blow a tire out in the boondocks, find a farmer with an almost new one, in a size big enough to fit the car, have a guy call his service station to put it on, and he don't charge you nothin'! I'll be damned," he said, laughing one of his huge laughs.

My favorite Cadillac story involves the owner of a small motel in our town. Everybody called him "Tweeter," apparently because of his high tenor voice and performances with a local barbershop quartet. In our small town there is one "respectable" motel. Another is about the same size, but it has a bar and topless dancers. There are two or three even smaller and older motels. Built during the dirty thirties, these would have been called tourist camps back then.

Tweeter's motel was clean, with small well-kept rooms. No restaurant or other amenities; just a simple, inexpensive place to sleep. Now, as it happened, a couple from New York City drove in late one evening and took a room. Tweeter's telephone switchboard lighted up immediately.

"Let me have room service," a women's sharp voice commanded.

"I'm sorry, ma'am, we don't have room service. May I help you?"

"You don't have room service? What sort of a sorry excuse for a motel is this?"

"There's a nice restaurant just two blocks down the street on the right," Tweeter said.

"That, I suppose, will have to do," she snorted.

When the couple returned following their meal, Tweeter's phone started its incessant ringing again.

"Why isn't the bed turned down?" the husband demanded. "Are these all the television stations you get?"

At this point, foundation must be laid for what occurred early the next morning after Tweeter had suffered a night of demands and insults. A very wealthy farmer from our community has a somewhat "slow" son named Franklin. The father recognized that after he was gone, provision must be made to take care of Franklin financially. He established a trust whose provisions assured Franklin of a new, top-of-the-line Cadillac each year. In addition, Franklin got a cash allowance of $1,200 each month, a princely sum at the time. Franklin's father did not foresee, however, what inflation would do to that amount. Soon, Franklin found it was necessary to supplement his income. He planted a huge vegetable garden and sold the produce door to door.

Meanwhile, back at the motel the next morning, the New Yorker drove his polished black Cadillac up to the office and came in to pay his bill. After complaining to Tweeter about the twelve-dollar cost, he gloated, "I'll bet you never see cars like mine around here, do you?"

It was at this precise moment that an overall-clad Franklin stumbled in and interrupted, "You wanta buy a bag of potatoes, Tweeter?''

''A hundred pound bag? Sure, bring 'em right in Franklin.'' Turning to the New Yorker, Tweeter pointed to an identical black Cadillac to his, weighted down on its springs with huge bags of potatoes.

''Yeh, we see a lot of those cars,'' he said off-handedly. ''Most people just use them for hauling produce though,'' as Franklin lifted a bag of potatoes out of the Cadillac trunk.

Later Tweeter confided that he certainly didn't have any use for 100 pounds of potatoes.

''Right then I would have paid a dollar apiece for them just to see the look on that guy's face,'' he laughed.

# 4

# *Learning the Ropes*

BY 1951 THE DECISION TO TRADE my '37 Chevy was not a hard one to make. Wrestling that vehicle down the road, I was reminded of the old farmer's admonition, "Try to keep her between the fence posts!" The car had a nasty trick in store for unwary drivers. At forty-two miles an hour it went into an uncontrollable, banging, shaking shimmy.

Shimmy was the scourge of car drivers of the time. The wheels would start an unceremonious back-and-forth vibration that would nearly shake the steering wheel out of the driver's hands. Of course, if you knew the beast, accelerating rapidly past that speed would often take one through the unseen barrier. By fifty miles per hour the old Chevy would lose much of its wheel-wobble and smooth out again—unless you hit a sharp bump. Then, be prepared for a wild ride indeed!

Vibration of the loose steering mechanism was worst at exactly forty-two miles per hour. The solution was to drive faster or slower. Of course, if the car went into a full-blown shimmy, there was no question but to slow down. The trick was to pass rapidly on through the critical speed, something like breaking the sound barrier in a jet airplane.

Worn tie-rod ends (the moveable parts which direct steering) or bad tires were often the cause of shimmy. Fittings called zerks allowed grease to be forced into steering parts using a pressure gun. They were supposed to be lubricated every 1,000 miles. Even at that frequent level the open zerks just couldn't keep grease in the steering parts. Driving on mud and gravel backroads and rural highways, or even on wet or snow-covered paved roads, washed out the bearing surfaces. Dirt soon contaminated what grease was left. Excessive wear and looseness was inevitable, as was the end result, shimmy.

With sufficient funds, I could have replaced all those front-end parts and temporarily corrected the shimmy problem. I didn't have "sufficient funds." I learned to live with shimmy. I assume that the once popular "shimmy skirts," worn by those marvelously undulating young women of the Roaring '20s, originated with front-wheel shimmy. There was even a popular dance called the Shimmy.

Surprisingly, I never had a wreck with the Chevy. I ended up in the ditch on several occasions, either as the result of heavy gravel and the loose steering mechanism, or because the brakes were so bad it was easy to get into situations where stopping or slowing down for a corner was impossible. When the brakes got wet, it was quicker to stop by "gearing down" with the manual transmission, or by dragging my feet. This was called "brake fade," which resulted from either overuse of the brakes or water getting onto the linings. Riding the brakes caused them to heat up, while water made them get slippery and lose stopping power. This made braking a real challenge on steep mountain downgrades, or anytime it rained.

On one occasion I narrowly missed a herd of horses that came up out of the ditch just over the peak of the hill. Stopping would have been impossible with those fade-prone brakes. Luckily, I just managed to steer through an open spot between horses, causing considerable panic among the herd and me. I became an advocate of disc brakes as soon as they became available on American cars, because of this, and other close calls I had due to poor braking. Discs solved most of the "fade" problems. As one man said, "They don't make cars like they used to—thank God!"

Another favorite trick of the Chevy occurred on hot days. Of course it was always necessary to drive with one eye on the temperature gauge. Nearly anything caused the car to overheat, even a prolonged tail wind. When the wind was behind you, not enough air was being driven through the radiator to cool the engine. This often meant an eruption of anti-freeze or the tap water which many of us used during the hot summers.

But on some occasions the car would simply burp to a stop from highway speed and refuse to start again, no matter how much I coaxed. In this case, cooler air was the cure. Opening up the two winged sides of the hood got the most ventilation to the engine.

Heat was the cause originally, so getting rid of as much heat as possible was the cure. The fuel had simply evaporated in the lines and caused an air blockage to the carburetor or fuel pump.

Logically, this condition was called "vapor lock." Until the car cooled down, which usually took twenty minutes or so, starting it was impossible. Sometimes, if water was available, I could pour it over the fuel pump itself to speed up the cooling process. If I was in a hurry, I'd have been better off taking a bicycle.

Chevy clutches at the time had a tendency to get rough and grabby. We certainly couldn't impress anyone with the smooth acceleration and power of our engine if we had a grabby clutch. The car would bump and jerk out of low into second, and bump and jerk again into high.

We drivers, however, had an innovative cure for the grabby clutch. We would simply run the bumper up against the nearest large tree, let out slowly on the clutch with the gear shift in high, and accelerate. A great deal of smoking and stink ensued. This method was not endorsed by mechanics, but it often worked as a cheap, but temporary fix. It "burned in" the clutch plates, sometimes removing the oil or what ever contamination had caused the problem in the first place.

A status symbol of the time was a steering knob fastened at about the four o'clock position on the steering wheel. These fit the hand neatly and rotated round and round. This made it possible to turn sharp corners using only one hand. They were designed to impress the opposite sex while keeping one arm around their shoulders.

Steering knobs were often made of simulated ivory on luxury models. The after-market knobs, like mine on the Chevy, usually had a near-naked girl enclosed under the plastic surface. This added to the ambience of the car. The less flamboyant had a solid hard rubber knob, in brown or black.

A major problem occurred if for some reason you lost your grasp on the steering knob during a fancy corner. The wheel would fly back around to its on center position very fast. If you were unlucky enough to have a wrist or an elbow in line with the knob on its return revolution. Hello, doctor, hello, cast. Let's get rid of that steering knob fast!

At the very least, you would be nursing a horrendous arm bruise for a few weeks. Steering wheel knobs weren't "in" for too long, for obvious reasons. They were replaced by gearshift knobs of roughly the same esthetic value. These, too, passed from the scene when manufacturers moved the long-stemmed floor shift up onto the steering column. This made a legitimate three-passenger front seat possible. Girls, especially, had balked at sitting in the middle of the front seat, straddling the old floor gearshift.

The male-female relationship was played out in countless ways with the automobile. A company called Burma Shave had an innovative idea for advertising their shaving cream. They spaced five relatively small, red signs with white letter-

ing about thirty feet apart along the side of highways. The signs were to be read in sequence and were always in rhyme. I remember one social comment specifically:

If necking on highways
Is your sport,
Then trade in your car
For a Davenport.
Burma Shave

Usually the signs involved safety. Motorists looked forward to the next grouping of the good-natured verses. Seeing how many different Burma Shave poems you could see and remember became a national pastime for many drivers.

Nary a man
Is now alive,
Who passed on a hill
At seventy-five!
Burma Shave

Whether the shaving product ever reached the popularity of the road signs is doubtful.

In the 1930s most of the narrow roads simply weren't good enough to permit higher speeds. In Nebraska, even the best of roads had a sloped curb on each side. Humorist Johnny Carson, a native Nebraskan, observed that apparently the highways were engineered this way to keep all the accidents in the center of the road.

From 1941 through 1945, the World War II years, the national speed limit was only thirty-five miles per hour. This allowed plenty of time to observe the countryside and read signs.

The wartime speed limit was initiated in the interest of conservation. What the government was conserving was rubber, not gasoline. The Japanese had taken over most countries who supplied us with the critical natural rubber for tires, while gasoline was a commodity produced in the United States in plentiful supply. Saudi Arabia's first oil well wasn't drilled until 1938, so Mideast oil didn't enter into the equation to any large extent.

Of course, the military buildup took vast amounts of gasoline, so rationing was installed. An "A" rationing card, meant pleasure driving only. It allowed enough coupons to purchase three to six gallons of gasoline per week. Not only were fines often stiff for violating the speed limit, you also could lose the valuable gas rationing coupons which were necessary to even be eligible to buy gasoline.

When the war ended, legal speed limits were raised and driving speeds increased. The novel Burma Shave ad campaign was outmoded. It became extremely difficult to read the signs as they flashed by. There was also some degree of danger when motorists lost concentration on the road, or slowed down to read the signs. In any event, the signs disappeared from the American scene sometime in the 1950s.

The heater was a major problem on most cars of the 1930s and much of the 1940s. It was a box-like object intruding into the lower right side of the passenger compartment. The metal case had small louvers on it. These were designed to direct the flow of heat. All heaters had a knob for setting the desired temperature level. The box also contained a fan. Fancier models had a two- or three-speed fan.

The one thing you could count on in cold weather was a need for plenty of blankets. If there were people in the back seat, they were certain to be freezing. The front-seat passenger was likely to have calves done to medium rare by the hot air from the heater. The driver, who couldn't avail himself of the blankets, or the direct blast of heat coming out on the front seat, simply had to tough it out.

We learned to dress very warmly. In particular, heavy wool socks, shoes, and five-buckle overshoes were appropriate. Not too good looking, but far better than frostbite. Too many Spartans had found what the cold winds swirling in around the holes in the floorboards could do to the unprepared.

''What holes?'' you ask. Holes for the brake and clutch pedal, a hole for the accelerator, holes for the choke, the throttle and the rusted-through holes.

All cars then came with a frequently used jack. Today, they still come with one, but it's likely you may not even know where it is. On today's cars you don't get another frequently used item: the crank. In cars built from the earliest days into the 1940s there was a hole at the bottom of the nose of the grill. When the battery, or starter, or generator or other part of the ignition system failed, which they often did, you could always crank the car to get it started. That is, you could always crank it if you had plenty of muscle and a good back.

The trick was to revolve the crank, which turned over the engine, while the ignition switch was turned on. This could be done by one person, since most cars had manual throttles on the dash which could be pulled out and set for higher engine speed. This provided a bit better chance at getting it started.

Someone at the wheel and someone on the crank was definitely the preferred method. A skilled operator could tell when the engine was about to catch and feed it an appropriate amount of gas. The correct hold on the crank was as important as that on your favorite golf club, in fact more so if you didn't care for broken thumbs.

Instead of grasping the crank handle between the thumb and fingers, as would be natural, the thumb had to be held back on the same side with the fingers. If the car backfired and the crank wasn't held properly and failed to disengage from the engine, the resulting surge would smash the crank into the hand, causing extreme pain and suffering. Think of all the potential automobile lawsuits consumer protection advocate Ralph Nader missed out on with the demise of the crank as a standard piece of car equipment!

Everything about my old Chevy wasn't antiquated. Take the "sound system" as an example. This was an AM radio, the only kind of radio station doing regular broadcasting then. The car radio was a "hang on" item, not being built into the dash, but hanging below it. A radio of any kind in a car of the vintage of the Chevy was considered an upscale option.

My radio was a box composed of vacuum tubes which not only got very hot, but consumed prodigious amounts of battery current. Driving down a highway, a properly working generator would continue feeding a charge into the battery, so the radio did not drain its power. Unfortunately, the old generators, as opposed to alternators that charge batteries in modern cars, allowed the battery to discharge at low speeds or idle. This meant that if both headlights and radio were on, and the car was driven around town at low speed, the battery was losing considerable power. It might not retain enough to start the car again when necessary.

Woe be unto the parkers who liked to create an appropriate romantic mood with radio music! Even if the car was left running at idle, the battery would discharge. If the car wasn't running, the radio didn't last long. It was too easy to get diverted and forget this important point. When the radio stopped playing, you knew you were in big trouble: Girls don't like to walk home.

More insidious was when the radio had been playing for an hour or so in some remote parking spot and music was still emanating from the single crackly speaker. As awareness of the situation came to the couple, there was often a hurried, "My Gosh! I've got to start the car!"

This was usually followed by a few grunts and moans from the engine as the battery gave up the last of its power. Options were limited. Jumper cables were unheard of, and it was highly unlikely you could locate another car anyway. You could try the dreaded crank, but it frequently wouldn't spin the engine fast enough to get it started. Both you and your friend could strike out on foot to look for the nearest assistance, or you could leave her sitting in the car alone for an undetermined period of time.

It was a catch-22 situation. She hated the humiliation of walking with you to tell somebody the car battery was dead (they knew what you had been doing). She was often afraid to sit alone in a dark car somewhere out in the boondocks while you went for help. Whichever option you selected was wrong.

If you were lucky, you might find a nearby farmhouse. Since the hour was often late you were almost certain to be met at the door by a disgruntled farmer you had awakened. He might have to get out the tractor to give you a tow start. Surprisingly, farmers often did this without charge. They could remember being in a similar situation themselves. They certainly weren't overjoyed about being routed out of bed, and if you got a real old one who had done his courting in a horse and buggy, you had to be prepared to pay considerably for disturbing his sleep.

Many cars had radios, but a high percentage of them didn't work. Car radio tubes were crammed into a box much smaller than the huge household console radios of the time. Therefore, excessive heat would literally burn up the tubes. Other parts were adversely affected as well. Car radio repair was a booming business.

My friend Verle had a part-time job repairing radios. He was also far ahead of his time in sound systems for cars. Verle was dissatisfied with the quality of sound produced by even the best car radios of the time. The broadcasts themselves were poor quality. The sound was further deteriorated by static, which was caused by everything from thunderstorms to any type of electrical interference, even from the car itself.

In the late 1940s, his solution was to take a forty-five RPM record player, which used seven-inch records, and build it into the glove compartment of his 1936 Plymouth. Glove compartments were much larger then. He installed a power inverter that changed six-volt battery current into regular 110 standard household voltage, and presto! Mobile recorded sound.

Verle could put a stack of forty-fives on the changer and have a half an hour or so of uninterrupted music that had much better sound quality than the regular radio. It was also ideal to impress friends while driving around having a beer or two in the car. (I'm just repeating what I have been told by others about this unlawful practice, of course.)

The engine of the car had to be left running in order to generate the proper power, but inexpensive gasoline made that a fairly cheap price to pay for better sound. The only problem Verle never licked was that the player arm would jump around if the road was too rough. It would skitter across the record making loud scratching noises, and often ruin the record. That problem wasn't solved for nearly forty years. Optional on many cars now is the laser beam CD player where nothing actually touches the discs.

This changer-in-the-glove-box was years ahead of its time. The automotive industry did not develop a satisfactory quality music system until the eight-track cartridge, and after that the much improved, smaller cassette tape player. In fairness, carmakers had to wait for technology to catch up. New electronics drew far less current than the old vacuum tubes and gave off much less heat. Transistors made an efficient radio possible, but even they had heat-related problems when first used in the small available space in a car dash.

The elaborate stereo systems in today's cars had to be delayed until integrated circuits, laser beams, computers, and huge improvement in small speakers could be developed. Technology has also nearly eliminated the associated maintenance problems.

Early on I learned about cars as investments. First of all, you have to do a lot more than just feed 'em gas on a regular basis. There are routine costs like oil changes or worn-out tires and batteries. You also must contend with less frequent maintenance items like sparkplugs or a change of anti-freeze. Actually, you can ignore any of these things, but at peril to your wallet. They always get you in the end with much poorer gas mileage, a plugged up radiator, or even serious drive train repair.

Major breakdowns from any cause are much more likely with older cars, say six or seven years, depending upon how they've been taken care of. That's just logical, of course. Mechanical things do wear out. A general rule is, "The older the car, the higher the cost of maintenance." Even then, an older car with its lower purchase price often turns out to be a true bargain, unless its owner dumped it knowing it had major problems.

As one car salesman told me, "Everybody thinks the used car salesman is out to screw the public by selling them junk. Let me tell you something. There's a lot more people out there trying to screw the used car salesman than the other way around. They'll tell him how good their trade-in is when they know damn well its got some real major problems."

He's probably right. Most of us normally honest, upright

citizens seem to undergo a complete transformation of character when it comes to trading in our own cars. We can look a car salesman in the eye and swear our car is one of the finest machines ever built, having just come from a mechanic who told us to get rid of that heap before it disintegrates!

Back to the cost of driving. When you're figuring costs on cars, you've got to add in insurance, taxes, licensing, inspections, parking costs, tolls, and a host of unexpected items. Even the novice car buyer soon recognizes these expenses in a hurry. Yet, we often forget the biggest cost of all, particularly on new vehicles: depreciation.

With depreciation, you reverse the rule "the older the car the more it costs." If you buy a new one, you lose nearly one-third of the car's value the day you drive it off the lot. Then its value drops to only about twenty percent of its new price over six years or so, depending upon make and model. That's why a used car is often the true best dollar value, provided you can avoid buying someone else's problems.

Somewhere about that six-year point, the resale value of the car depends almost entirely upon its condition. How does the paint look? Does it start and run flawlessly? Is it a popular car with young people or collectors? Is the interior clean and sharp? Has it been wrecked?

All these things make a big difference in the car's actual worth. Also, about the sixth or seventh year is the time the costs of ownership once again evens out. Much of what was saved on the purchase price may very well have to be spent on major repair and maintenance bills over a period of years. Still, with all things considered, about one-third of any new car is strictly an owner prestige expense.

One of the first things to remember when trading is to get an established price on the vehicle you want to buy before you talk about trading in your car. If the salesman pushes you about it, tell him you haven't decided. You may sell your car outright, and perhaps you will. Get a cash price on the unit you're trying to buy. If you don't, you're one of those buyers car sales people call a "pilgrim" or a "laydown," both uncomplimentary slang terms regarding your buying sense.

Don't pay any attention to what a car salesperson tells you about how much "trade-in" you'll get on another car. He or she might just inflate the price of the car you want to buy to make you think you're getting a fantastic price for your present vehicle. Would a used-car salesman do that? Do flashy blondes like Corvettes?

Would we believe what we're told about that super trade we're getting? Of course we would! There's a sucker born every minute according to P.T. Barnum. Who can resist a fantastic bargain? Not most of us.

I learned about the true value of most older used cars when I wanted to trade in my '37 Chevy. Since I was newly married, we needed more dependable transportation. I soon found a one-owner, chalky gray-white 1940 Nash. It was a major step up in car condition, despite the large spot on the back seat that looked like half a gallon of ice cream had melted there.

The car had several of the unique features I had seen in Nash's advertisements. In addition, the tires were better, and most important for my new responsibilities, it had "overdrive." Overdrive was simply a fourth forward gear that could be engaged automatically from third by simply lifting the foot off the gas pedal. The car would shift, providing less power, but also using considerably less gas at highway speeds. Aha! Justification for buying this vehicle.

I had a little trouble trying to figure out to how to start it the the first time. Mr. Peterson, the car dealer, handed me the keys. I searched the floor for the starter button. Nowhere in sight.

"Just push in the clutch, son," Peterson told me. "Safety feature. You can't start her in gear."

There beneath the clutch pedal was the small starter button. Neat!

"She's got a great ride. Smooth as silk," he assured me.

In fact, that was about the extent of his sales pitch. I drove the quiet car for a few blocks and was ready to buy, but I wanted to be sure I would get a good trade-in on my Chevy.

I had paid $150 for that car, and ten times that much in maintenance. I wanted to get my money out of it. To Peterson's credit he explained the rules of car trading in the most direct manner I've ever heard.

"This fine 1940 Nash sedan is going to cost you $400 cash outright, or $550 if you still think you have to get a $150 trade in for your old Chevy."

"The Nash needs a paint job," I pointed out, disappointed at the nonexistent value of my car.

"O.K." Peterson said. "If you take the Chevy to the junkyard and the battery's any good, you can probably get about twenty dollars for your car. I'll just knock that off the price."

"But that doesn't help the paint on the Nash any," I protested.

"Tell you what I'll do," Peterson said as he chewed on his unlighted cigar. "I'll paint it for eighty dollars."

I still didn't have the money. "But that's allowing only twenty bucks for my car!"

"Son," he said, "It ain't worth more than twenty dollars. Maybe somebody will paint the new one cheaper and save you some money. $380 is cheap for that Nash."

"I'll have to think it over."

"Better not think too long." He took the cigar stub out of his mouth and pointed at the Nash. "Somebody's always looking for a good running car like this one."

He knew I was going to buy the Nash long before I did.

# 5

## *More Good Deals*

MY IMMEDIATE CONCERN was coming up with the money. Peterson was helpful.

"How about making it in four equal payments, over the next several months?" he asked.

This no-interest deal was probably one of the things that made me a long-time customer. The other was that Walt Peterson, and later his son Gene, started out with a fair asking price on the vehicle in question and rarely came down much from that figure. Normally, after some shopping around, I'd find that the original quoted price really was fair. This first Nash purchase was more or less the start of a car-buying relationship I had with that dealer and that make of automobile over the next twenty years.

All this was in the days before factory window stickers on today's new cars. The Nash I was buying then was about ten years old, so stickers wouldn't have entered into it, but it bears making a point in passing. Most window sticker prices you see today are genuine reflections of the suggested factory retail pricing. Others are fake "look-alike" factory stickers with a "creative" price put on by an unethical dealer. These show an exaggerated base price and extra equipment that may not be on the vehicle. After all, how can you tell if the car has the special road handling suspension shown on the window sticker? You can't see it. That is illegal of course, and car manufacturers do their best to control the few who try to get by with the tactic.

Others often include a second window sticker listing an additional dealer charge. This is not illegal. When I shop for a car and see a "pack," as it's called in the industry, I head for the door. Who knows what other "cost enhancing" methods that dealer is using? A typical pack sheet includes additional phony charges, such as special undercoating, finish sealer, dealer make-ready expense, upholstery soil protectant, or other items, apparently limited only by the dealership's imagination.

Getting back to my immediate concerns with the 1940 Nash, I needed to find someone to paint it cheap. That chalky grey white and rust brown needed a lot of help to be suitable family transportation. Fortunately, my friend Verle (the guy with the forty-five RPM record player in the Plymouth glove compartment) had an idea. His father had been employed as a painter at the old Kearney air base, and when it was closed he had "liberated" some large cans of paint, mostly dark air force blue.

Painting conditions were not ideal. The garage where we worked had a dirt floor and poor lighting, but Folke Straatmann was used to working under less than ideal conditions. It was to be a forty-dollar bargain paint job, just half the price I had been quoted. Things went along smoothly through the sanding process that several of us were helping on. We did not, however, give any thought to taking off *all* the old paint and primer. Only in a few places where a small amount of rust showed did we do that difficult work.

Then came the magic day when the Nash became midnight

blue. That is, it appeared to be midnight blue until after it had dried and we backed it out into the sun. Then it was something like a multicolored Easter egg, ranging from a gorgeous deep blue to areas of grey-blue and light blue.

Folke Straatmann allowed that it didn't look too bad. I hated it. He knew it.

"Let's give her another coat," he suggested.

It actually took several coats before the car became an even midnight blue, one that both Folke Straatmann and I agreed looked "nice."

From this little experience I learned something about repainting cars: *Never paint a dark color over a very light color.* I still didn't realize, however, that the opposite is just as true. Never paint a light color over a very dark one, unless you are planning on multiple coats.

I found an old Nash manual and some sales literature in the glove compartment. I learned that the car will "flash you from fifteen to fifty miles per hour in less than thirteen seconds, in high gear. Then simply engage the fourth speed forward and save up to twenty percent on gasoline." Ah, yes, they were ahead of their times. A gallon of regular gas cost about thirty-five cents back then. Unleaded, or "white" gasoline as we called it, cost about twelve cents a gallon.

See anything strange about those costs? Most cars needed the leaded regular to lubricate parts and protect valves, so we never ran unleaded in a car engine. Unleaded also induced more "ping" or engine knock. Since the demand was for regular leaded gas, it cost about three times as much as unleaded. This is a tribute to the principle of supply and demand.

Along this same line, I had been employed by radio station KGFW as an announcer and salesman while I was still in college. One of my accounts was a filling station owned by a gentlemen named Howard Nims. Howard was a jocular, round-faced little guy who did a pretty good business at his filling station. (This was before they were called "service stations." Now they're mostly "non-service stations.")

Regardless, Howard was having problems with his profit margins and wondered if there was anything we could do to help him raise his earnings on gasoline sales. He said that he made a lot more money on premium or ethyl gasoline, but that it hardly paid him to have a pump with ethyl in it because so few cars needed it.

The full technical name for the gasoline additive is tetraethyl lead. It is a colorless compound added to gasoline to increase power and prevent knocking. The product also forms the base for common alcohol, ether, and many other substances. Higher levels of tetraethyl lead were essential in certain high compression engines, which perhaps ten percent of the cars on the road had. Whether it improved performance in any way for the other ninety percent of the cars *not* requiring it was debatable.

Our ad campaign bordered on the ridiculous. Each commercial started out the same: "Your friend, Howard Nims says," and then launched into something like, "come on down to the station and try a tank of Nims Ethyl gas. Your car ain't gonna fly 'cause it ain't got no wings, but you're gonna think it's about to. Remember, one tankful of Nims ethyl gas and you'll never buy regular again!"

I sometimes took even crazier approaches, ranging from obviously exaggerated claims to poetic nonsense, to a form of reverse psychology. For example, in the middle of winter when cars were starting hard anyway, I came up with something like, "Your friend Howard Nims says, 'I'll bet you're glad you filled up with Nims ethyl gas last night instead of regular. In fact you can't even buy any regular from Nims today—all my regular gas froze up overnight! Guess I'm gonna hafta cut down on the water I have to add in order to make a decent profit on regular. Well, you know you oughta have Nims ethyl gas in your car anyway—so come on in. We got plenty of Nims ethyl in the pumps, and it ain't froze up yet!' "

Within a period of weeks Howard Nims was mighty happy with his ad campaign. Instead of Nims ethyl gas accounting for about five percent of his sales, it now outsold regular nearly three to one, and he had a lot of new customers who would just stop in to rib him about his radio spots. The strange thing is, after writing hundreds of these commercials way back then, I don't even remember what brand of gas Howard Nims sold.

However, I decided that even my flights of fantasy in the Nims radio ads couldn't compare with much of the car advertising of the time. Listen to this direct quote from Nash sales literature I found in the glove compartment of my latest car purchase:

> You'll see it pass like a ship in the night . . . a silent blur . . . a silver phantom. And you'll know by the sudden thump in your pulse—you've seen your first 1940 Nash!
>
> But when you take the pilot's seat, hold on tight! For there's more power under this flashing hood than you've probably ever toed before. A touch on the throttle . . . and the country outside becomes a crazy-quilt. Then a Fourth Speed Forward seems to shoot you

forward on the giant shoulder of a wave . . . but here's something new: When that car looms up ahead, give the throttle an extra nudge and you'll feel a spurt of power that leaves him in your wake a mile behind. It's Nash's new automatic overtake.

Exciting? Yes—but WAIT! Head for a road that's full of bumps. Then watch the hood ahead. See if you can make it bobble—try to feel a rise in that air cushion beneath you.

With a baby's grip on the wheel, you can feather it around sharp curves . . . make it walk a chalk-line on loose gravel, or a soft shoulder. Outside there's a frosty wind stripping the trees—but you don't feel it. Nor will you ever know cold, dust, or stuffy air again—thanks to the new wonders of the Weather-Eye.

You are having your first Arrow-Flight Ride, and if you can't get that proud hood headed homeward tonight—just pull up—beneath a scarlet tree—and turn down your Nash convertible bed!

Five minutes in a new 1940 Nash is more fun than a lifetime in ordinary cars, yet a Nash is as easy to own as any. Big as it is, it's priced with the lowest.

Now that's glowing prose! Actually, the Nash I had, with the L-head six cylinder engine did have ample smoothness, although its 105-horsepower engine and 3,300-pound overall weight didn't exactly give the car "more power than any you've ever toed before." Its price new was somewhere around $1,000, so it held its retail value very well indeed. Although the sedan was a bit stodgy, it had a 121-inch wheel base, very large by today's standards.

The car moved with us to Chicago when I went into the air force. In fact, the first major problem with the car occurred in the middle of busy Mannheim road on the east side of what is today O'Hare International Airport. At that time, during the Korean War, O'Hare was simply a military base.

One evening after duty, in the midst of full rush hour traffic, the Nash suddenly locked up both rear wheels at about forty-five miles an hour, screeched, and smoked to a stop. It's rather amazing that I didn't create a twenty-car pile up. What had happened, I learned later from the mechanic who towed the car to a nearby garage, was that a pin in that much-heralded overdrive transmission had broken and locked up the transmission, ruining it altogether.

We couldn't locate another overdrive transmission. Nash only built about 10,000 of these cars, so we ended up with junkyard standard gears and a car that never ran as well, or as efficiently, again.

Sometime prior to my owning the 1940 Nash, my father had switched his allegiance from General Motors cars to Nashes. His first new car was a 1947 Nash 600. It was called the 600 because that was how many miles it could go on its twenty gallon tank of gas. It was large, yet lightweight, being a "one piece welded body and frame," to quote from another Nash ad of the time.

It was able to hit that thirty-miles-to-the-gallon, provided you didn't push it too hard on the highway. Fifty miles an hour was about right. The 600 had a top speed of only seventy, which made passing on two-lane highways a thrill. It took a long time to get from fifty to seventy; longer than my eyes could see.

Comfort was a big selling point for cars in those years. The Nash had coil springs on all four wheels to "erase" bumps. It was a vast improvement over the rough riding pre-World War II cars.

Dad did not buy the Nash for its ride or fuel economy, so masterfully described in its advertisements. He bought it because that was the only new car he could get without being on a very long waiting list. The World War II conversion of car plants to the manufacture of military equipment caused the shortage of new cars. Some people by-passed these lists of buyers by offering extra money under the table. It was a sort of car black market.

The Nash dealer did not take bribes. When your name came up, you got a car. Dad liked that attitude.

This Nash had back doors that opened from the front, just like most Fords, Studebakers, and other cars of the time. Some people called them "suicide doors."

Dad was proud of that new Nash. After all, it was his first brand-new car. This was before I owned my first car, and I well remember trying to borrow that new vehicle.

"Dad," I said, late one Sunday afternoon. "The church youth fellowship group is having a joint meeting over at the Newark church south of the river. Nobody's got any transportation."

"Uh huh," he said, in his best noncommittal manner.

"We sort of made plans to go, but P. E. couldn't get the car."

"Uh huh," he said.

P. E. was a kid nobody could stand. He lied about everything and anything for no apparent reason. He combined mendacity with a surly, bullish stupidity. However, he often had a new vehicle available through his father's car dealership.

We disliked him so much that our lack-of-a-car crowd would draw lots to see who had to call P. E. to make transportation arrangements.

I got the short straw earlier that afternoon.

"Hello, P.E.? How ya doin'? Got the car tonight? No? . . . Well, see you around, P. E."

The situation had become desperate. Otherwise, I would never have asked to borrow dad's three-day-old new car.

"It's about ten miles over there," I said. Too far to walk in other words. Dad knew what I meant.

"Who's going?"

"Just Wayne and Dave, and . . . uh, probably three girls from youth fellowship."

"How long does the meeting last?" Was this the third degree or what?

"Gosh, I don't know, Dad. Couple-three hours I guess."

"Hmmmmm."

It was all over now. I could tell by the tone of that last *hmmmm*. To my surprise he reached in his pocket and handed me the keys.

"Be careful with that new car. Just over to the Newark church and back home as soon as it's over."

"Sure, you bet, Dad!. Soon as it's over. Great! Thanks, Dad."

I couldn't believe this good fortune. Not only did I have a new car to drive, we didn't have to listen to P. E.'s wild babble. What's more, we could probably have our choice of the three best-looking girls in youth fellowship, maybe even the preacher's daughter.

If you didn't live through that period of time, you may find it difficult to understand why a stodgy four-door sedan would impress girls. There simply were very few new postwar cars of any kind available then, so four brand-new wheels were definitely prestige transportation. That was about the way it turned out. Girls practically lined up to go with us. Six of us made our way happily to the new car.

To the south of Kearney is the Platte river, "a mile wide and an inch deep." It makes for some long bridges. To cross the river at this point, we had to take a 1920's vintage bridge, a narrow span that allowed two-way traffic, barely, and not if one was a truck. It had silver iron posts with large knobs at each connection imbedded in a concrete understructure. Usually people treated the bridge as if it were one-way. Whoever was on the bridge first had the right of way.

We were all in high spirits. As was the custom with parties of six, the boys were in the front seat and the girls, giggling about something unknown to us, were bouncing around in the back seat. It was getting dark, so of course I had the headlights on when we reached the old bridge. I edged on it at about thirty-five miles an hour, arriving far ahead of the cars at the other end. The first driver in the line at the other end apparently wasn't familiar with our one-lane bridge custom. He pulled onto the bridge, followed by the other cars.

"Oh no!" I thought. "Hold her steady and slow," I told myself. "There's no problem." I white-knuckled the steering wheel.

"Ignore the back seat commotion," I thought. Suddenly there was a screeching crash and a stomach-churning smashing of glass. I fought off panic. I didn't dare look around to see what was happening, as I was concentrating entirely on keeping the car in my own lane. The original heart-stopping racket was then followed by intermittent thuds of metal on metal.

I had no place to hide, as more traffic approached. I braked, but by then we were nearly off the bridge.

As soon as I could speak I yelled, "What in hell is going on?" at the preacher's daughter and her friends.

"Ardis opened the back door while we were on the bridge!" one of the girls said meekly.

"She *what*?" I couldn't believe it! "*Why*?" Dad's brand-new car! I wasn't three miles from home and I had already wrecked it.

We stopped on the shoulder. Only then did I realize that after Ardis had opened the rear-hinged door and it banged against the bridge posts, she had continued to hang on to it. Her hand was welded to the door handle as tight as mine had been to the steering wheel. If the door had been ripped off, she would have gone right with it. As it was, she was terrified but unhurt.

At that point I wasn't thinking about positive, important things. I was thinking about what I was going to tell Dad when I got home with his new car. How unlucky can you be? It wasn't even my fault! I was a dead person.

I took everybody back to the church and then headed home for the lengthy reprimand I expected.

I presented the wreck to Dad, including the gruesome details. After he inspected it, he asked, "Nobody's hurt then?"

"No, but I thought about killing that dumb girl."

"Well, son, accidents can happen. We can get the car fixed. We're just lucky the car was so strongly built that the door didn't come off."

I knew then how much I loved my father.

My own 1940 Nash had some mechanical troubles of its own by 1951. My wife and I decided that it would be best to try to locate a different used car and trade it off. Our gas mileage had gone to pot without the overdrive, the car had new noises of undetermined origin, and both rear tires had worn flat spots from the locked-wheel stop it had made when the transmission froze up.

Our first stop was in a downtown Chicago dealership whose ad we had seen in the newspaper. It was our first experience with high-pressure selling tactics. This is where used car salesmen earn their low reputations, only a notch above lawyers according to some surveys. We got the "bait and switch" technique. That's where the quoted price on a particular model that was "just sold" turns into the same car at a much higher price.

We got the low ball, the fake discount, and the "I'll have to clear this deal with my manager." When all these failed, we were handed over to a full-time, high-pressure "closer." Sales contracts were pushed in front of us. We were told we had to sign, since we had already made a verbal commitment. My wife got so nervous she decided we should just keep the old car.

I was also intimidated by these tactics. Then I thought back to the time when I was in high school and had taken a girl to a carnival that was in town. I had just gotten my paycheck from my part-time job at Sears and we hoped we were going to have some fun. A man in a skimmer hat pointed his cane at me from behind a counter and said, "You look to me like a winner!"

I felt pretty good about that, being with the girl and all. So I stepped up boldly to the counter and plunked down the quarter the man said his game of chance would require. He rolled around a number of balls and proclaimed me to be the winner. I didn't understand the game, but he gave me fifty cents and asked me if I wanted to go again. Are you kidding? Of course I wanted to go again.

You can probably guess the rest. All I really remember him saying each time he pushed those numbers around was, "The only way you can lose now is quit or drop dead. Oops, that'll cost you fifty cents, but the only way you can lose now is to quit or drop dead."

I didn't do either. I ran out of money. "Sorry you lost," he smiled. "Just to show you my heart's in the right place, here's a dollar back. You and your girlfriend have a good time, ya hear?"

I hadn't had that terrible feeling, like I was really being conned, again until right there in that Chicago car dealership. I wasn't going to let it happen again. We escaped to a small suburban dealer and found a human being more like the kind we were used to.

"We may have just what you're looking for," the salesman said. "Got this very low mileage 1949 Ford coupe. Great looking car. It was owned by a little old maid schoolteacher who just used it to drive back and forth to work and to church on Sundays."

"Sure, and pigs can fly," I thought "How many of these guys can you run into in one day?"

"It's true," he said, seeing the look on my face, "Here's her phone number. Go talk to her if you want to."

We looked at the car first. It seemed to be as clean as he had said.

"Seafoam green," the salesman said, referring to the color. "Listen to that baby purr."

"How much difference?" I asked.

"That your old Nash over there?"

"Yes. And a fine dependable car it is. Always starts."

"Hmmm. We don't get much call for Nashes." He flipped through the pages of his sales book. "Tell you what. We'll just take $1,100 and your car."

Ardelle and I looked at each other. "Let's talk it over," she suggested.

"Fine," the salesman replied, "but don't think it over too

long. You won't find many cars like this one.'' Somehow, that sounded familiar. Is there a nation-wide correspondence course that teaches cliches to car salesmen?

I called the teacher. ''About forty is as fast as I ever drove it,'' she assured me. ''Runs real good.''

''Why did you trade it off?'' I queried.

''I trade for a new car every three years. Bought a new Plymouth.''

That was good enough for me.

''This is the model that saved Ford from bankruptcy,'' I told Ardelle. ''Real popular car.''

''It seems pretty nice,'' she agreed, ''but it's sure a lot of money.''

''Maybe he'll come down,'' I said.

We went back to the dealer. ''We'll give you $900 and our car,'' I said.

''Let's split the difference,'' he reasoned. ''An even $1,000.''

We became the owners of a Ford that was considered a ''driver's car.'' It was a neat little package that had been designed for Ford by moonlighting Studebaker designers who needed some extra cash. It was a good car. Much later I learned that this three-year-old Ford had cost only $1,500 brand new!

We took it out on the road for a drive. It ran flawlessly up to forty miles an hour. Then it bucked and snorted and refused to run more than about fifty. I was incensed.

''The damn thing doesn't run right,'' I told the salesman.

''OK, OK, Not to worry. We'll take it back in the shop and fix it. No charge.'' This was more the kind of service I had expected.

But after they worked on it, the car still didn't run much better. ''Tell you what,'' the chief mechanic said. ''I think it just needs the cobs blown out. Take it out and run it wide open whenever you can and let's see what happens.''

I did as he suggested, and gradually the top speed increased.

Within a few days that Ford would zip right up to seventy-five and ran like a top. The only problem we never could get corrected was that whenever it rained we had a trunk full of water. Seems that the acquarium-trunk was a very common problem with 1949 Fords.

In the meantime, I got a couple of quick military promotions and Ardelle's employer gave her a raise. Within a year we were in the market for a *real* new car.

# 6

# *War Stories*

A LARGE AMOUNT OF PRESTIGE and self-satisfaction is found in owning a new car. At least it seemed that way to me when we made the decision to buy our first new vehicle. Our '49 Ford had developed an engine miss, which several shade-tree mechanics diagnosed as bad valves.

Since we had owned the car only a little over a year and a half, and since it had been such a faultless road performer, I considered having the engine overhauled. The more I thought about this prospect, the more time I had to listen to the siren song of new car ads. Traditionally, new cars of all makes were introduced during one short period in September and October.

Model changes being made during the Korean war were largely cosmetic, or some minor hyped-up engineering change. Regardless, all makes of cars had their elaborate new model "grand showings."

I was so psyched up to purchase a new vehicle, I didn't give a thought to other possibilities. I must have been in approximately the same state of mind as the air national guard pilot who flew his F-89 jet in for a landing at O'Hare, the Air Defense Command base where I was stationed.

Normally, my job didn't allow me to spend much time down on the flight line where the action was. I worked in the large brick administration building, much like any other office building. On this particular afternoon, Lieutenant Miller was officer of the day, generally a pretty dull job at a stateside air base not directly involved in combat. He wanted a few hours of company while he made the rounds in his jeep.

We were cruising along near one of the alert hangars when the radio in the jeep crackled to life. The voice was from the control tower to a fighter jet that was on final approach to landing.

"Angus 2450, your wheels are not down," the voice said, "If you have a malfunction, please advise immediately and take another go around."

The airplane was equipped with a safety device that sounded a very loud horn in the cockpit if the pilot got below a certain altitude and the landing gear had not been lowered.

More urgently now, the voice of air traffic control came on again, "Angus 2450, I have you on visual and your gear is not down. Repeat, your gear is not down."

We began heading out toward the runway where the plane was coming in. Now the tower was screaming, "*Lower your gear 2450, lower your damned gear*!

The plane continued its approach and settled in for a beautiful landing, followed by a terrific racket and showering of sparks. In a surprisingly short distance the jet had arrived at a full, perfectly straight stop. Emergency vehicles with sirens blaring were heading out from the fire station, but our jeep was the first to reach the scene.

The shaken pilot had already climbed down from the wing and was heading away from the plane in case there should be a fire. Lieutenant Miller and I ran over to him.

"You all right?" Miller asked him.

''Yeah, I guess so,'' the ashen white face replied.

''Didn't you hear the tower yelling at you to lower your landing gear?'' Miller demanded.

''I couldn't hear anything in that cockpit for all the damned noise that horn was making!'' he said in his defense.

That's about the way it was with me wanting to buy our first new car. I couldn't hear anything that made good sense for all that damned advertising that was blaring at me.

Sometimes, when models required almost no assembly line changes, cars would be held for several weeks or more in a dealer's back room, carefully covered from eyes that might see them before their release date. This strategy had been very successful, primarily because of the auto shortages immediately following World War II. Major design changes were made in cars soon after the war, which also helped promote the unveilings.

During the 1953 model year, we went shopping for our first new car. It was also the last year we bought a car that could be considered only basic transportation. Our selection was severely limited by our available dollars. We obviously were not going to buy much beyond an entry level vehicle, so our goal was to get a model with the most ''standard'' equipment possible.

There were few foreign cars sold, except for elitist models such as Rolls Royce or Mercedes Benz. Foreign cars were a minor factor in the U.S. auto market then. On occasion you might see an MG or a Volkswagon, but during the beginning of the Korean War patriotism had soared, like it does in every war. Buying a foreign-made car was considered unpatriotic.

A car purchase in 1953 represented about one-fifth the cost of a modest new home, and modest homes then sold for $10,000 or less. Our limit was about $2,000, plus the value of the '49 Ford for which we had paid $1,000 a year-and-a-half earlier. Despite my previous experiences with the trade-in value and depreciation of used cars, I still convinced myself that this would add up to us being able to afford a car up to about $3,000.

There weren't many automotive test reports available to the prospective new car buyer then. The first owners report questionnaires were conducted by Floyd Clymer, a well-known automotive writer. These were not driver-test reports with objective evaluations. Clymer sent out 1,000 questionnaires to car owners just to see how well new cars had lived up to expectations. His owners' surveys became a regular feature of *Popular Mechanics* magazine in 1950. Which car was the subject of the very first report? One of my own favorites, the Nash Rambler.

And which American-made car do you suppose got the highest owners satisfaction rating during the first twenty years of the owners' reports? The 1955 Packard, with a ninety-seven percent excellent rating. Other highly rated cars were the Buick Roadmaster of 1954, the 1965 Ford Falcon, and the American Motors Rambler and the Pontiac Tempest of 1966. Owners said they would definitely buy these cars again. Isn't it strange that none of these vehicles are still being built? There should be an asterisk in that statement though. Buick has dredged up the Roadmaster name again and applied it to a 1992 vehicle, so the name, at least, is not totally dead.

Tom McCahill was another widely read car-tester. He wrote automotive reviews for *Mechanics Illustrated* magazine in 1953. Big Tom's reports were highly subjective. He tested only the cars he wanted to test and used a seat-of-the-pants driving approach.

The only thing vaguely scientific about McCahill's tests were his mileage estimates. He used a "fifth wheel," a device resembling a motorcycle wheel dragging behind the car, and a gauge to correct for the ever-present speedometer errors. Using a measured one gallon of gas, he would then see how far he could drive before the engine quit. This wasn't too accurate, since variables such as wind, heat or cold, wet or dry pavement, or how heavy McCahill's foot was that day weren't considered. Tom made up for all his disregard of objective testing with puns, good humor, and at times disparaging remarks aimed at certain automobile manufactures.

At that, his methods may have been at least as accurate as those EPA gas mileage figures of today. Those are the numbers you find displayed on new car windows and touted by those companies who finish high in the annual rankings. There's plenty of reason to suspect the accuracy of these mileage figures. You've probably noticed that they show a city driving figure, and a highway driving number.

Why is it we rarely attain these figures in our own driving? It's all in the way the tests are run. Does the EPA take the car out on a test track, load it up with typical family paraphernalia, and simulate the actual conditions encountered in day-to-day driving? No, that would be too simple. The government stages its mileage tests indoors on a dynamometer, a machine that places the car's driving wheels on rollers. The car isn't actually moving, the movement is merely simulated.

Tom McCahill's subjective methods were at least entertaining. He had a built-in bias for very large, very fast, American cars. He was a solid 250 pounds plus and his personal choice was the huge-finned Chrysler 300C, a car that featured a conservatively rated engine that produced more than 390 horsepower. That's right, 390 horsepower—not cubic inch displacement, torque, or some other fanciful number to describe an engine.

It was a hemi-head model with a high ten-to-one compression ratio. This Chrysler used a new torsion bar front suspension rather than coil springs. The famed Vigil Exner was the man behind this brute force model. It fit Tom McCahill to a "T".

I doubt that McCahill ever tested anything as mundane as the 1953 Plymouth or comparable cars I was considering. Evaluation of all new cars hadn't even been considered at the time. Drivers didn't have even crude figures for mileage and performance for most models.

Couldn't we find help by reading *Consumer Reports Magazine*? Sorry. This was before the days of overall model surveys of in-use problems. There were no "best buys" listed to let us know what independent testers thought to be the better values in cars. Most certainly there was no chance to study the dealer's actual cost in an attempt to arrive at a fair price.

And there were no tips to help us spot a shady dealer. We found that out the hard way when we had walked onto the lot of that high-pressure outfit in Chicago. In short, caveat emptor.

The only basic guide available was a rule of thumb. The bigger the car, the more it was going to cost. If a car weighed more, you paid more.

Unfortunately, in the throes of new car buying frenzies, reason often escapes the brain. The media was full of seductive new car ads. In fairness, they didn't use as many glamorous female models to peddle the cars as is done today.

In a typical ad, the Car was pictured right up front. Usually there was a "typical family" somewhere in the near background. Ads extolled the virtues of lasting fashion and a solid investment in the future. We were all quite naive about buying new cars in those days. There was no "lasting fashion." Cars depreciated rapidly, as styles changed.

Because I had written a considerable amount of ad copy in my radio work, I recognized the psychology. The instant passing power of the Pontiac "Strato-streak" or the Oldsmobile "Rocket 88s" were hot buttons to the prospective buyer. So was the '55 Chevy "Turbo-fire" V-8. GM seemed to have the most imaginative descriptions of their big V-8 engines, although Ford was the first American make to use V-8 engines on a wide scale. When GM hit the market with an engine to replace their old straight-eights and sixes, they did it in a big way. Big engines, big carburetors and big advertising budgets.

Several cars were available with a newly designed roof, a sporty looking innovation that had no center pillar between the doors and the roof. This was called a hardtop (distinguished from a rag top) convertible because it gave the look of a convertible with its top up. Better judgment told us that this design would weaken the car's structure considerably and result in squeaks and rattles. It turned out that the hardtop should have been called the squash top because of its propensity to flatten in rollover accidents. Safety considerations caused the hardtop's demise.

It didn't take too many trips to various dealers to learn that (1) The trade-in value of our Ford was less than half what we had paid for it, and (2) We couldn't afford one of the new overhead valve V-8 engined cars. That was what I really wanted. We settled for a more sedate 1953 Plymouth flat-head six. This was the same model still in use as the taxi cab of choice in Cuba almost forty years later. At least we recognized durability when we saw it.

We chose the Cranbrook model, a step above the lowly base-level Cambridge. The price: $2,340 dollars, less our $440 trade-in. (How did we lose more than half the value of that '49 Ford is just eighteen months?) We were left with just about enough to pay the taxes and license fees. The car was a two-tone brown and cream and boasted more chrome than the cheaper model. It had a three-speed manual transmission with the shift lever mounted on the steering column. None of those optional new-fangled automatic transmissions for us. We knew they would never hold up, and besides, they cost too much. Our car was a four-door sedan, a concession to future family considerations. An AM radio and a better grade cloth covering the bench seats were our only "luxury" options.

But, it was a *new car*. I expected some sort of recognition from my colleagues at the air force base. Unfortunately, the same day I arrived at the base with my new Plymouth, another guy from my outfit with a much fatter wallet, or better credit than I had, showed up with a flashy new two-door, sport-trimmed Rocket V-8 Oldsmobile. Nobody even noticed I had bought a new car.

I had always heard you can't eat prestige, but I thought that only applied to jobs. When I worked at KGFW radio and it was time for a raise, the boss would shake my hand and offer his heartfelt appreciation for a job well done. Sometimes I received a new job title, also without additional pay. When that failed to satisfy my desire for more money, the station owner offered to put my picture and title on a new set of advertising blotters. "Think of the prestige of being pictured on a genuine, widely used, KGFW blotter," the boss said. No raise, of course. He eventually did come through with a pay hike, and I never was pictured on the blotters.

The Plymouth was a family car that served us very well indeed. All we had to do was change the oil and grease it, put gas in the tank, and drive it. Parking wasn't the easiest because it had no power steering. The brakes were standard non-power types, but at least they were on all four wheels. In short, the car was "practical." But like all new cars, if you look at my purchase from a dollar-and-cents standpoint, I was long on dollars invested and short on "sense".

Shortly after my first new car purchase, I had become friends with a new airman third class (the next to the lowest air force rank). Bob Novack typed the morning reports each day, which were accountings of actual on-duty status of personnel at the air base. Bob was a native Chicagoan. His father was a personage on the Chicago Mercantile exchange. Like most of the rest of us college boys, Bob was a draft-dodger, enlisting in the air force only to avoid being drafted into the army. This seemed to be the easiest route to the completion of military service requirements, short of joining the national guard. "Overqualified" as a morning report clerk would scarcely describe him. Bob spoke fourteen foreign languages. Every morning he took a bus from his home on the lakeshore to work, and then again took one for the long trip home each evening. He was getting pretty sick of it.

"Know anything about cars?" he asked me one morning.

"I've owned a few," I admitted.

''That's not what I meant,'' Bob said patiently. ''I mean, do you have a pretty good idea of what's a good car?''

''Well, you knew I just bought a new one, didn't you?''

''Really?'' Bob looked at me suspiciously. There I was, deflated again. ''Is it exactly what you would have bought, regardless of price?''

I had to admit that it wasn't. I really wanted that up-scale V-8 I couldn't afford.

''What's so great about a V-8? What's that refer to anyhow?'' Bob wanted to know.

''It's a type of engine. Eight cylinders, four to a side in a kind of V-shape. Got a lot of smooth power.'' How could a guy be fluent in fourteen foreign languages and know nothing about cars?

''OK. What new model would you buy right now?''

That was a tough one. ''There are a lot of good cars, but I really like that Chrysler New Yorker I saw over at the Des Plaines dealer.''

''Would you drive me in to see him over the lunch hour?''

''Well, sure. I guess so.''

So it was settled. I was Bob's resident expert on car buying. We drove the five miles or so into town and walked into the show room. Of course, since it was the lunch hour we both had on our air force uniforms complete with our minimal rank indicated on the sleeves. We walked in and began looking at the cars on display.

The three salesmen on duty took one look at our uniforms, an obvious sign of no money, and ignored us completely. If there weren't bars, oak leaves or eagles on your shoulders, sales people often thought it a better use of their time to drink coffee or read a magazine than attempt to sell something to a serviceman. I even recall seeing some signs in business establishments in Chicago, ''No Dogs or Airmen Allowed.''

''What's this green and white one?'' Bob asked.

''That's the new Chrysler, the one I was telling you about, only this one is loaded with extras.''

''Like what?'' he wanted to know.

''Well, it's got the big V-8 engine, of course. Looks like its got power steering, and an automatic transmission—that's the little lever there on the dash.'' It was an unusual location for the automatic shift lever. The lever pointed straight out at the driver and was an obvious safety hazard. The position was changed very soon.

''Anything else?''

''Yeh. This one's got power brakes and it even has air conditioning!'' A portion of the air conditioning unit was mounted in the trunk. Large, clear plastic tubes came out of the rear shelf and pointed toward the front. Chilly ears were in store for rear seat passengers.

''I like the way it looks,'' Bob said. ''I think I'll buy it.''

''Wait a minute, you don't even know how much it costs,'' I reminded him.

''Well, let's find out.'' The sales force was still pretending to do something—anything—else, rather than waste their time with a couple of poverty-stricken military people. Bob and I bypassed the salesmen and walked over to a receptionist at her desk.

''The boss in?'' Bob queried.

''No, I'm sorry—wait a minute, he's just coming in now.''

''What can I do for you?'' the owner asked.

''I'm thinking about buying that Chrysler over there,'' Bob answered.

''You mean the green and white one?''

''That's the one. How much is it?''

''Well, just a minute and I'll figure out the monthly payments,'' the owner said.

''No,'' Bob corrected him, ''I mean what's the total price?'' This was before the days of window stickers, so we really had very little idea of the car's retail cost.

''I was just looking at the invoice this morning,'' the owner said. ''I think it's $5,600 and something.''

''OK.'' Bob replied. ''Can you have it ready to go by four-thirty this afternoon?" That was when Bob got off work.

"Uh, . . . sure. I think we could work it in. Just how did you want to pay for it?"

"How about a check?" Bob asked. "Can we just call it $5,600 even?" he said as he continued writing in the amount.

"Yeah, that's OK. What bank is the check on?"

Bob turned the checkbook around. "Oh—Mr. Novack—the stock exchange Novack. Yes sir, no problem!" the owner said with obvious surprise.

If his was a look of surprise, you should have seen the stunned expressions on the faces of three salesmen, who each missed a chance at probably their biggest and quickest commission sale of the year.

In all likelihood, I was going to be transferred overseas to someplace like Greenland, Saudi Arabia, or Newfoundland. I had been on orders at various times for all those places. Each time the assignments had been cancelled, for reasons known only to the military minds. I had been told I was indispensable to the operation of the base. Imagine, a lowly enlisted man working at various jobs which technically did not even exist on that base, being indispensable! In this situation I could never be promoted.

Apparently this indispensable business had come from the fact that at the base commander's request I had spent several months of research, writing something called "The History of the 83rd Air Force Squadron." It so pleased my superiors that I got a letter of commendation, and absolutely no increase in rank, or pay. It was KGFW blotter-time all over again.

Then my military career started on the upswing. I had "cross-trained" into a new job classification which was authorized at our base. Then came three rapid promotions, mostly thanks to my years of suffering at low pay grades. I was sent to a short three-week technical school, quickly passed the required tests, and got an assignment as head of a new on-job training department, with almost limitless enlisted rank open above me. When the base commander waived my "time-in-grade" requirements, I went zooming up the enlisted pay scale.

Ardelle had also become an inspector on her line at Baxter Labs. We had no medical expenses to worry about, being military. In short, it seemed like a great time to have a baby.

Some women seem to look and feel absolutely sensational for at least the first four or five months. Ardelle was sick for nine months. We did wonder at the time if it had anything to do with her doctor's name, Dr. Staysik. I believe, this might be one of the rare instances where a name change would be professionally beneficial; and for the chiropractor in central Nebraska, Dr. Grosshands. (A Mr. Outhouse, from Loup City, had long since changed his name to Owens.)

We were looking forward to a wonderful, caring time during her pregnancy. But Ardelle started heaving up her socks, couldn't stand the sight of food, and lost twenty pounds from her already thin body. But she forced herself to continue working, stopping only on the way to work to open the car door and be ill by the side of the road.

I empathized with her situation more than she realized. Growing about four inches around the waist was a bit strange considering how little we ate, and the fact that I wasn't the one who was pregnant. I had to buy a new uniform as my twenty-nine-inch waist increased. Fortunately I lost most of that girth within a month or so, although Ardelle's ordeal didn't improve, despite all the medical help we got. I soon got sympathy morning sickness, to go along with her all-day sickness.

She needed the car to get to her work, which left me sharing a car pool. The driver was a master sergeant who left for work long before sunup so he could stop by a bar near the base and have two cups of coffee each laced with a couple shots of whiskey. Just watching that didn't help my morning sickness.

As far as the pregnancy was concerned, we had no knowledge in 1954 of such modern practices as birthing chairs or Lamaze classes. Husbands in the room during labor and present at the actual birth? Not unless it was in somebody's taxicab on the way to the hospital!

When it actually came down to baby delivery time, our first run was a false one. That was largely because we were about twenty-five miles, through heavy traffic, from the military hospital. At the first twinge of possible labor, I insisted we take off. We needn't have worried. When the real thing occurred, it was hours of difficult labor in a hospital so overcrowded that Ardelle didn't have a room. She had to share a cold hallway with several other pregnant women.

Of course, I couldn't be there with her. She was in misery, and I was having a nervous breakdown. The staff nurses got tired of my pacing the floor and asking them to check on things every five minutes. Finally, after about twelve hours of this, three off-duty military nurses took pity on me, or their fellow nurses, and sat me down for a nervous two-or-three hour pinochle game and a continuous flow of calming information about having babies.

Finally it was over. The nurses were very anxious to get me in to see my wife and the new daughter they told me we now had. They had given Ardelle considerable pain medication, and the baby wasn't cleaned up much when I first saw her. In fact, I was shocked.

"That's not ours," I told the nurses. "You have made a mistake." It certainly seemed logical amid all those babies in the nursery. The infant was a dark, purplish color with lots of messy black hair. (A "blue" baby, we later learned.) The closest thing I had seen to this creature was in the Lincoln Park Zoo. She seemed to be screaming constantly and the red and purple face indicated an undetermined origin. Perhaps even outer space. One would never have guessed that this reluctantly claimed infant would become the light of our lives in a few short days. Despite her demanding start, Vicki, named after my father, would become a very self-reliant and attractive young woman.

There was another occasion, a number of years further down the road, when I decided something else just couldn't be mine. We had ordered a new 1967 model car, the first sight-unseen purchase we had ever made. Automotive brochures always use a certain amount of artistic license when depicting the vehicle they are selling. In this case, our new car bore little, if any, resemblance to the artist's conception I had chosen. When the supposedly gold-colored Nash appeared, I went to the dealer's to sneak a peek. The car had just come off the truck, which had apparently been through a mud storm. There were some unexpected styling changes that were most unpleasant—minor, but detracting from the good-looking, popular lines of earlier models.

The interior was solid black, an idea that had sounded good when the order to the factory was placed. The strange color combined with a few added pounds of chrome not on the previous year's model caused me to say, like I had with my firstborn, "That can't be ours!" It was. Unlike Vicki, the car did not show vast improvement as it got older. We were stuck with the beast for four years.

We continued to drive the '53 Plymouth for several years after my four-year military enlistment ended. The only major problem we ever had was an "act of God."

No, not like the acts of God at the cathedral in Mexico City. There, Saturday afternoons and early Sunday mornings, cars are parked all around the huge square. Hoods are open, legs stick out from underneath, interiors are being worked on by their owners. There they wait until a priest comes by to shake holy water on their car and bless it. From the looks of many of those vehicles, most are past the point of normal repair, so divine intervention is probably the only hope. (However, that doesn't explain the durability of those Plymouths in Cuba. Under Castro, Cubans are officially atheistic.)

Our personal "act of God" was two-fold. We had just

rounded a corner on a highway in western Nebraska late one night. My eye caught something at the top of my headlights. I was driving about 50 MPH, which was the speed limit at night at the time, and we were about to meet a truck. I braked hard, but too late. An enormous truck tire crashed into our Plymouth with a tremendous roar. My wife and baby daughter were on the right front side as the tire bounded on up over the car taking the windshield wiper with it. It was that close, yet it didn't break the windshield or hurt any of us. That was the first act of God.

The second was when I approached the owner of the truck the next day. He said he didn't think he was liable for such an occurrence. He had obviously already talked to his lawyer. Although my insurance company would pick up the damage, I didn't want to pay the deductible, or have this charged against my policy and trigger a raise in rates.

I consulted my own barrister.

"Get back to you tomorrow," he said.

When he called the news wasn't good. "I've found several cases that offer precedence for the act of God argument," he informed me. "I think if we have to go to court with this thing, you'll probably lose."

"Wait a minute," I said, "Somebody's got to be responsible for a rear dual coming off that truck."

"Seems like it, but all the cases I could find say an act of God involves an unavoidable accident and a blameless owner."

"So what do you suggest we do?"

"Bring suit against most of Scottsbluff County," he laughed. "Sue everybody from the owner to the driver to the manufacturer to the last guy who changed the tire, to the people who serviced the vehicle and anybody else we can think of."

"And then what?"

"I expect somebody will get nervous, think this could turn into a major lawsuit, and put some pressure on their insurance

company to settle the property damage and get a total release signed in a hurry."

And that's exactly what happened. The car was fixed and there was no real structural damage, just a lot of repairable expenses. In addition, I had to pay the legal expenses to my attorney. I didn't really believe that "act of God" business. Why would God pick on me?

Since I was using our Plymouth to go to work every day, we realized the need for a second vehicle. I spotted a 1948 Packard four-door sedan for sale by the owner. He wanted $175 for it. In its day, this had been quite a car, probably Packard's best of the era. It had a huge 396-cubic inch straight-eight engine and something called "ultramatic drive." This was not a true automatic transmission, since the car had a clutch pedal, but you could shift gears without using the clutch when you had the "ultramatic" engaged. The guy who was trying to sell the Packard called it a semi-automatic transmission. I thought that was probably a lot like being semi-virginal.

The car had sold new for about $4,500. Even though it was eight years old, because of the low asking price, I suspected problems of some type. The car had typical Packard luxury and was reasonably clean. But, sure enough, the engine had a suspicious miss in it. Since it was only going to be used around town, I offered him $150 for the car and he took it immediately.

The Packard became known in our family as the "Where's the baby?" car.

With the arrival of our second daughter, it was a hectic time for my wife. She was planning to spend an hour or so with other new or expectant mothers and had hurriedly loaded all of the typical baby paraphernalia, plus a playpen into the Packard. Then came a diaper bag, a bag of toys, and other baby essentials. Our two-year-old daughter was crowded in, standing back of the front seat.

Ardelle drove away in great haste with her huge payload, when the two-year-old asked, "Mamma, where's the baby?" A hurried return trip found her still at home, asleep in her crib.

# 7

# *Floozies and Doozies*

OUR '48 PACKARD could be best described as elephantine. It weighed well over two-and-a-half tons and rode on a 127-inch wheelbase. The metal in its fenders alone would have been enough to build the entire bodies of some of today's thin-skinned beauties. In fact, you probably could have parked most of them in the distance between the wheels of a Packard limousine. That car had a 148-inch wheelbase.

One of the most striking Packards of this vintage I ever saw belonged to a man whose wife could be called "frugal." Harvey had surprised the Missus one day by showing up at home with a new, gold, limited anniversary edition Packard Eight. To those who knew Harvey and his domineering wife, it was a marvel that he survived that little surprise.

It wasn't that they didn't have plenty of money, they just weren't in the habit of spending any. Either Harvey had entered his second childhood, or he had run across a salesman of amazing ability.

Harvey's routine driving habits didn't change with the purchase of the gold Packard, however. He refused to park anywhere in the downtown area where there were parking meters unless he could find a meter with time left on it. On one particular trip to town Harvey and the Missus had been circling a several block area, passing up several choice empty spots that had no time on their clocks. After all, twelve minutes cost a penny. (Apparently the expense of the wasted gasoline never occurred to either of them.) Finally Harvey's wife spotted a meter with considerable time left on it and Harvey wheeled the Packard into the spot.

After completing their shopping, they returned to the car with more than ten minutes to spare on the meter. Harvey started the car and began to back out of the space. The Missus stopped him. She insisted that the car stayed parked until the time on the parking meter expired. Now *that's* tight.

Not one who wanted to be considered "frugal," as soon as I got a job promotion the decision was made to keep the '53 Plymouth as a second car and send the Packard to a retirement home for dowagers who weren't functioning on all cylinders. Then we would buy a new vehicle. My lawyer bought the Packard for about one-third of what we had paid for it. He thought he stole it and I thought he deserved it.

I never liked having a vehicle I was sure to meet on the street a hundred times a day. The problem was that I really couldn't afford the rarified costs of automobile individuality. Therefore, I narrowed my new-car search down to two cars: the 1957 DeSoto, made by Chrysler Motors; and the huge 1957 Nash Ambassador. Both of these cars were excellent choices for distinctiveness. Sales were so low that this was the last year of production for the big Nash, and the DeSoto had only token production for three more years until it also became extinct.

The DeSoto and its sister car, the Chrysler, were nearly exact duplicates under the skin. However, they had about the same relationship in appearance that a hooker has to a

socialite. If the DeSoto had been a woman, she would have been adorned with a blonde wig, huge earrings, purple eye shadow, fake eyelashes, and bright orange lipstick. She would have worn short-shorts, black fishnet stockings, and red five-inch high heel pumps.

There was no question that the styling of the DeSoto lacked class, but its ads were even worse than its looks. One ad pictured the huge tail fins from the rear angle and the headline, "This Baby Can Flick Its Tail at Anything On the Road!" Then at the bottom in large print, "DeSoto," followed by tiny lettering, "the most exciting car in the world today!"

The DeSoto's sibling, the Chrysler, was a socialite and highly fashion conscious. She wore any style as long as it was expensive and haute couture, regardless of how well it suited her shape. They didn't call her "the New Yorker" for nothing. I couldn't afford the classy sister's taste.

The Nash had a slightly different look about her. The basic style originated in 1955 with a fairly straightforward, somewhat aerodynamic design. It was powered by a small, but powerful Packard-built V-8 engine. Nash wasn't prepared for the fickle public's switch en masse to V-8 power plants. Nash's own V-8 made its debut with the 1957 model I was considering buying.

The 1955 design was still used. The headlights were mounted in an oval grill making the car appear to be about three-feet wide at night, something like a big sedan version of the Austin Healey sports car. The car was a two-year styling aberration, but in the process of correcting that odd look, the new model sacrificed any attempt at form following function.

The Nash reminded me of an eye-catching ad an insurance company was using at the time. It showed a picture of a house which had been added on to at least a dozen times, with an equal number of different architectual styles. The caption read, "You wouldn't build a house without a plan, why buy your insurance that way?"

I should have applied that thinking to car buying. There were certain similarities between the Nash and the DeSoto. The DeSoto was called a "Fireflight," while the Nash was named an "AirFlyte." Each car had exactly the same rated 255-horsepower engine, which was coincidental because the engines were built by their respective companies. Each had glitzy, wide-spaced chrome strips on the side pointing toward the front of the vehicle. They widened as they separated and continued to the rear taillights. Between the chome was a third color.

The '57 Nash looked like a car built by a congressional committee and passed on for Senate-House compromise. It had so many amendments you couldn't tell what it had been originally. The car had a giant oval, heavily chromed grill with a large golden "V" and the round Nash emblem at the V's point. This was to highlight the new Nash V-8 engine under the hood.

It also had a fantasy version of an older Nash hood ornament last seen on the 1955 models. That ornament featured a busty woman with chromed flowing hair. It reminded one of a metallic version of the old wooden figureheads on the prows of sailing ships. The woman's figure wasn't eliminated in the new ornament, but had been stylized. The designers apparently took two ornaments and threw a heavy chrome oval ring around them. The thing must have weighed eight pounds.

There were four stacked headlights, a new styling innovation shared with the Lincoln of the same year. Then, topping the front fenders, were parking lights in two-foot long chrome bezels running lengthways of the vehicle. The show car was grey and pink, with pink and black plastic and cloth upholstery. This eighteen-foot long behemoth had "lightning stripe" chrome strips the full length of the sides outlining the pink trim.

The front wheels were exposed, so the car had a much smaller turning radius than the earlier Nash models in the late forties and early fifties. Chrome was two inches wide and everywhere. The windshield was called a "wide-wide Scena-Ramic." It was one of those that folded around back into the front doors and made terrific knee bangers. The trunk of the car continued straight back into two gigantic oval taillights, housed in, of course, chrome. The car had one-foot tall backup lights that were bright enough to light a football field. Backup lights were found on only a few cars at the time. To their credit, Nash did not succumb to the huge tail fins that were so much in vogue. That fad had been started by Cadillac in 1949, and simply grew in size with other makes until the fins got totally out of control, particularly with Chrysler products.

The hubcaps on the Nash Ambassador were giant chrome circles with six-inch red-and-black Nash emblems emblazoned on each. The whitewalls on the tires must have been four inches wide. White wall tires were an extra cost item then, while black walls are often higher priced today. (The American supply and demand system strikes again.) Door handles appeared to be taken from another Nash division, the Kelvinator refrigerator.

The steering wheel was black, with a huge chrome center and chrome-plated circular horn ring. The seats in the Nash had to be among the widest on any car ever built. The car looked like it could hold an entire baseball team in reasonable comfort. Under the padded black dash was a huge expanse of, you guessed it, genuine burled chrome.

No question about it, I liked the style.

The 1957 DeSoto or the 1957 Nash could be bought for about the same $3,000 straight-out cash. This was nearly $1,000 less than the suggested retail price of each. Even so, the price of all cars, with their extra comfort equipment, was now equal to approximately one-third as much as a modest home, instead of the twenty percent our new Plymouth had represented four years earlier. Since there was relatively no inflation those years, the only explanation was more and more extra equipment options, which were highly profitable to the manufacturers.

Both the Nash and the DeSoto were huge cars. Both had air conditioning, a true luxury item at the time, and twin AM radio speakers. (This was before stereo or FM in cars.) Several things finally swayed me to buy the Nash. I had read independent reports on unit body safety that were very favorable. The Nash was built with a unit body, the DeSoto wasn't.

"Twice as strong—twice as lasting—assures top resale value," the Nash ads said. They also had a method of "rust-proofing" their basic unit body structure by dipping the entire car body in a huge vat of primer paint.

The Nash "Weather Eye" was the best ventilation and heating system on the market. In fact, it had recently been traded to General Motors in exchange for "Hydramatic." Nash needed an automatic transmission in the worst way, because they had misjudged the public demand for that feature. The patented reclining seats still made into "twin travel beds." Nash was modestly called, "the world's finest travel car."

No question, the new V-8 engine had plenty of power, and

the four-wheel coil suspension made for a smooth, if somewhat nautical ride. That was the norm for the big American cars of the times. Car manufacturers apparently felt you should always slow way down when you came to curves in the road.

We had made a profit when we sold our home, so we bought the Nash outright with cash, no trade-in.

In today's environment of long-term warranties, it seems unusual that there was almost no consideration of that item in new cars then. Some of the better manufacturer's warranties covered defects for ninety days following purchase. One car salesman described his product's warranty to me, only half-kidding, "You buy the car, and its fully warrantied until you drive it off the lot!"

That's much like an acquaintance used to tell clients who had bought health insurance policies from him: "You understand this waiver don't you? The policy won't pay for anything that the waiver excludes. Some policies have a huge list of ailments that are excluded. Yours has only one exclusion. See right here? It says it will pay on anything except the skin—and its contents." Fortunately, he was joking.

In practice, most car dealers stood behind their products informally and would fix most minor problems out of their own pockets. Major factory goofs were often paid for, at least in part, by the manufacturers. That was not something you could count on, however. The never-ending string of expenses often associated with a lemon were basically the buyer's expense after the first few months. I learned all about that with my new Nash. Although it wasn't yellow, that '57 model came as close as any vehicle I ever owned to being like that bitter fruit.

The first big surprise was gas mileage. About twelve to thirteen MPG was absolute tops on the open highway. Only three or four miles to the gallon was average around town.

The first time we took the car on a major trip, another couple went with us. When we traveled in those days, the normal arrangement was that the car owner paid for all routine maintenance expenses, such as oil changes and grease jobs and tires. We were almost certain to replace one or two tires on a long trip. In addition, the car owner paid for any and all unexpected major repair bills, and that wasn't an unusual occurrence out on the road either. In return, the other couple paid for all the gas.

Our friends thought that was eminently fair. We traveled from Nebraska to New Orleans by several scenic routes, then back into Texas at the eastern border. We toured through Houston, and eventually went down to Brownsville and across the border into Mexico.

We visited some Texas relatives, headed west, and after some extremely long travel days, ended up in El Paso. The next morning we headed north. We soon realized that the state of Texas really is bigger than most countries. Going north through the panhandle we still had about 500 miles to go to get out of it. It seemed to us that Western Texas is composed to a large extent of miles and miles of nothing but miles and miles.

We alternated drivers, but our feet got heavier and heavier on the accelerator pedal. Soon eighty-five seemed to be the normal speed, but there were still Texans in pickup trucks passing us. Then I looked down at the gas gauge. It was time to fill up the twenty-two gallon tank. Charley paid the bill, and then he drove for a while.

"My God! This thing's dry again." He filled it with gas once more.

During the third stop that afternoon, I walked around to the rear of the car just as Charley was pretending to stuff five-dollar bills into the gas tank. "Might as well avoid the middle man," he said wryly. Luckily, gasoline was only about thirty-five cents a gallon then. At today's prices, he would have had to use twenty-dollar bills for his little joke.

"Look at the bright side," I told him, "Think of that surge of power you feel when you step down and hear those extra two barrels on the carburetor open up on that big V-8."

"Sounds like you're flushing the toilet," he agreed.

No car would give decent mileages at those high rates of speed, but we must have averaged seven or eight miles to the gallon. The sad thing was, we were still used to the twenty MPG of our Plymouth.

My friend Charley was an extremely likeable guy who had gone through very large amounts of money on various entrepreneurial ventures. One attempt at big-bucks-business came when Charley decided to go into the house-moving profession. He didn't approach business like most people might, starting out slowly and hoping to grow.

Charley bought the biggest and most expensive house-moving equipment available, guaranteed to move anything. The tracked vehicles with their huge hydraulic jacks and leveling controls were state of the art.

When he got his first request to relocate a building, it was a doozie—a huge old three-story house with an enormous porch on two sides. Unbeknown to Charley, the owner had been trying for several years to find a company anywhere in the region who would take on the job. Nobody would.

"No problem," Charley said. "We've got the equipment and crew to handle it. We just have to find a route that has wide enough streets and get the power and telephone companies to raise lines. That will be the major problem," he remarked confidently.

Charley's crew went to work raising the house onto huge timbers and bracing. They dug below the house to get the crawlers underneath. It was here that the crew hit its first trouble. The house was sitting on a pool of gooey muck that had apparently been caused by years of rain water accumulating without having a ready escape route.

"No problem," Charley assured his customer, "That's why we bought these expensive tracked movers instead of trying to use wheeled vehicles. They've also got all that extra weight we're going to need for stability''.

The digging continued until all four crawlers were strategically placed under the enormous moving timbers. Things were all set, but it was too late in the day to begin all the road clearances and electrical work the city had to handle. The big move was set for 5 A.M. the following day.

Unfortunately, that night is still remembered as ''the night of the big rain.'' Three- or four-inch rains are fairly common on the plains once or twice a year, but that night the deluge reached nine inches.

Charley rushed to the moving site at first light. Water was standing level all around the house. Charley's new equipment was beneath it all.

''No problem,'' Charley observed. ''We'll just get some pumps and suck the water out of there, and in a day or so it'll be dry enough to make the move, if the water hasn't ruined the engines.''

At that moment, the house gave a gigantic shudder as one corner sank at a precarious angle. Then another heaving groan as the whole side slipped into the hole. Soon the huge old house had squatted and sunk down to its original level, burying Charley's new moving equipment underneath.

''No problem,'' Charley told the anxious home owner. ''You don't owe me a cent.'' The startled man didn't know what to say. ''We'll just leave those crawlers under there for extra stability and if you ever want to take 'em out, you can have 'em!''

That ended Charley's foray into the house-moving business.

My experience with the '57 Nash wasn't nearly that expensive, but probably more frustrating because of the four years it dragged on. Every week something else would go wrong. The dual-exhaust system needed replacement mufflers and other parts on a regular basis. The famous Hydramatic transmission leaked, soaking the garage with fluid. It required a major replacement housing, and later, a total overhaul as well. Then the valves in the engine went bad and had to be ground.

Even the pink and gray paint faded. I opted to have the car repainted white over the darker colors, which had become a horrid eyesore. On an earlier car I learned that a dark color should never be painted over a light one. This time I had simply reversed the process with light over dark. The results were just as bad. It meant another expensive lesson and more coats of paint.

I wouldn't have spent money on repainting except for the conviction that I had already paid to have everything fixed on this vehicle that could possibly need to be fixed. My mistake. There were more disasters waiting in the wings.

Spark plugs continued to burn up about every 7,000 miles, regardless of the heat range of the plug selected. The distributor required constant repair, and even though the four-barrel carburetor was rebuilt twice, it was still frequently out of adjustment. The air conditioner failed regularly. In desperation, I had the air conditioner clutch spot welded so that the system ran all the time. In winter, the air conditioner belt was disconnected and the system did not operate at all. This corrected most the failure problems, but then there was the Nebraska weather pattern. It's summer one day and winter the next, or vice versa. I needed a full-fime repairman.

The new tubeless tires on the Nash were troublesome because of excessive wear, tread separation, and sidewall bulges. They needed to be replaced frequently, and tire warranties were much more limited then than they are today. Usually a tire dealer would go to his book for an "adjustment" price. This was a jacked-up retail price approximately double the "sale" price for which you could buy the tires outright anytime. If the tires had any sort of miles on them, say two or three thousand, the dealer would use his tread depth gage to determine the amount of wear.

The man who developed this system must have received the industry award as moneymaker of the decade. The tread gauge was placed into the spot on the tire with the shallowest tread depth. Since the tire was defective from the factory, that meant that spots were usually worn unevenly, reducing tread depth in those places. That's where the tread was always measured. It had also been determined by the tire manufacturers that an unusually large percentage of new tire tread wear occurred in the first 2,000 miles the tire was on the car. Therefore, even if the wear had been relatively even before a tire failure, drivers still paid for an inappropriate amount of use when the tread depth guage was used to determine the cost for warranty replacement.

"Looks to me like this tire is about half worn-out," the tire man would say as he looked studiously at the gauge. "Yessir, down to 6/32″ tread depth. But, we can fix you up."

That was for sure. After this double talk he would quote a price only slightly higher than the cost of the tire without any "adjustment." Obviously, if you were dealing with a local tire company, the warranty was more likely to mean something. However, it seemed that tires forever went bad somewhere far away from home where the salesman could use the tread gauge routine and there wasn't much you could do about it.

Defective tires couldn't be blamed on the car, except to the extent that the '57 Nash front end could not be kept in proper alignment. It was more than a nuisance, alignment was considered routine maintenance and a costly routine at that.

Perhaps my '57 Nash was the poor man's Jaguar. Recently an acquaintance in Omaha sold his Jag. Since it was less than a year old, I asked him why he had parted with it.

"Great looking car," he confided, "Tremendous prestige automobile. Everyone should own a Jaguar at least once just so it can be parked in the driveway where friends and neighbors can see it. Jaguars are absolutely superb art objects. Then you need another car for driving."

"You mean it's not a good road car?" I asked suspiciously. Jaguars were known to be very smooth and powerful vehicles.

"That's not it at all," he said. "Damn things just spend most of the time in the shop for repairs rather than on the road. Two friends of mine had the same experience with theirs. Beautiful cars though. We all hated to sell them."

Unfortunately with my Nash, I had all of the expense without the beauty.

My boss Milford's car experience was a doozie of a different sort. His new car drew considerable attention around our office because of its candy-apple red color and macho design. No question, it was a beauty. Milford had spent a number of months studying various models, test-driving them, and narrowing down his selection.

Then he bought a list of manufacturer wholesale prices, dealer mark-ups, and other data that he felt would put him in a better bargaining position. He narrowed his selection to three different makes that met his specifications. Next he hammered out what he assured us was the best deal anyone had ever gotten on a new car.

He may have been right. In his own case he certainly was, since it was the first new car he had ever purchased.

That evening Milford was scheduled to work with one of his salesmen, who would normally have driven his own car.

"Let's take my car," Milford said magnanimously.

The pair drove out to make the sales call that evening. It was slightly after dark when they arrived. The client's house was located on a calm side street in a small city.

Milford looked over the area carefully for the best parking spot. An old pickup was sitting in the street in front of the house, so he decided it would be best to stay away from that. He drove on and parked two doors farther up the street, where there were no cars around that could nick his polished chrome bumpers or scratch his glossy new paint. Milford carefully pulled in very close to the curb, set the parking brake, even though the street was very level, and the pair went into the client's home.

Milford and his salesman were in the middle of an excellent

presentation when suddenly they heard a loud *thump* and a shattering of glass. Could something have hit the old pickup out front?

Everyone went outside. There sat the aged pickup with no sign of damage.

"What the heck do you think that was?" Milford asked the couple.

His salesman answered that question with another.

"Hey, Milford! Where's your new car?" Sure enough, it was nowhere to be seen. It had disappeared from its lonely parking spot about fifty yards away.

Milford took off on the run. He was horrified at what he found. In the next block was a huge wad of tangled metal of the same color as his new car. On the opposite side of the street facing the same direction was a dilapidated vehicle with its entire front end destroyed. Inside sat an older man and a young woman, dazed but unhurt. Both were uproariously drunk.

Milford called the police who came at once. They arrested both people, who were still sitting happily in the remains of their vehicle.

"A block," Milford mumbled. "He knocked my new car a whole damned block!" He arranged to have what was left of his car towed away.

Early the next morning Milford hurried down to the police station to file the accident report. He learned that the man's name was Twiddle Two Sticks.

"How about his daughter? How's she?"

"Soon as she sobered up we let her go. But, hey, she's not his daughter. That's Vida White Eyes. She's one of our regulars in here," the officer said. "The other thing you're not gonna be happy to know is that I checked with Smiley's Used Car lot and the old guy's got no insurance on that heap he was driving. Then just to top it all off, his driver's license expired a couple days ago."

Twiddle Two Sticks had taken his fifty-three-year old wife

into the local hospital for major surgery. Once she was through it successfully, he was so happy he decided to celebrate. He did this in no uncertain terms. At some place he couldn't remember, he crossed paths with Vida White Eyes, a twenty-some-year old barfly. Then he proceeded to drive erratically around town, apparently at a very high rate of speed in an attempt to impress her. That's how he met Milford's new car.

Milford decided to go back to the cell and talk to him.

"Actually, I secretly planned to kill him," Milford confided later.

Twiddle Two Sticks was very hung over. When Milford explained that it was his car that had been hit, the old man said how very sorry he was.

"I sure didn't mean to get all carried away and do that," he apologized. "Ruined *my* new car, too," he said. Milford had seen what was left of the rolling junk yard the man had been driving.

"You just bought that car?"

"Just yesterday after the wife come through the operation so good. We needed a car, bad. I was so happy." He looked sadly at the floor of the cell.

"Why didn't you have any insurance on it?"

"The salesman said I did. Said he'd take care of it. Said I had full coverage." Twiddle Two Sticks sighed in misery. "I gave that fella all the money I had and he said it was enough for the car and the insurance—'cept for the ten bucks I saved out to celebrate."

"And the girl. Who's she?"

"I dunno. Got too much rotgut in me. She ask to go for a ride in my new car. I'm really sorry." He rolled his eyes. "Please don't tell my wife, Mister. I'm already in the dog house now since I ain't got the money and no car either one."

"What'd you do to Twiddle Two Sticks, Milford?" we all asked the next day when he told the story at the office. "Are you going to file charges against him?"

"Aw, hell. I gave him a hundred bucks and told the old

coot he better keep his nose clean or he'd have to answer to me. He's in enough trouble already."

"What about your new car?" someone had nerve enough to ask.

"My insurance company says they'll pay for it, except the deductible." He thought about things for a moment. "You know, this might not have even happened if it hadn't been for that floozie. Twiddle Two Sticks might have just passed out somewhere when he finished celebrating and be up at the hospital smiling at his wife right now," he mused.

"So what kind of new car are you going to buy now?"

"Haven't decided," Milford said wryly. "I hear the army will make me a hell of a deal on a surplus Sherman tank."

The crowning blow with my floozie, the Nash, came when another of the car's frequent problems, oil use, was diagnosed this time as bad piston rings. There were only about 60,000 miles on the odometer. This bad news was on top of the fact that strange internal sounds in the newly designed V-8 were almost a cinch to be major trouble, possibly bad rod bearings.

After just four years, the Nash had cost me a fortune. Furthermore, when it was in the shop, one of us didn't have transportation. Ardelle didn't care for that. Obviously, we were going to buy another car. I decided to trade for a simple automobile that didn't have all that new-fangled equipment to break down.

Although I did shop the market, I finally decided to stay with my Nash dealer, who now sold Ramblers, since the demise of the Nash brand. The major reason for this loyalty was that he had certainly tried to make things right. More importantly, he was willing to accept my trade of this big, extinct monster, for a normal-sized vehicle. Other dealers weren't interested. Although the Rambler's new price was far less than my Nash had been, I still took a financial beating.

Nobody really wanted a car that wasn't being built anymore. Nash combined with Hudson and became American Motors. At that point, their new vehicles took an entirely different approach to the motor car, based on the small, efficient car design of the Rambler. This was out of sync with the big-car times, but the Rambler developed a group of very loyal owners.

When a car company goes out of business, merges, or stops making certain models, the original car buyer loses money fast. There is a slightly different method that has the same result. Here are a couple of 1992 examples. The British-made Sterling and the French Puegot are both good cars, but the manufacturers recently discontinued selling the cars in the United States. Any guesses on what that does to the resale value, or how costly and difficult it will be to get repairs in the event you tried to just drive your money out of them?

There's a lesson here. Watch for information about how your car manufacturer is doing. If they are in a downward spiral in sales, and their stock plummets at a greater rate than their major competitors, it might be wise to get rid of that make before its resale value disappears. Frankly, I'm an expert at watching the value of cars I've owned evaporate, so pay attention—maybe even take notes!

# 8

## *Playing the Horses*

WHEN A NEW HORSE RACING TRACK opened in our section of the state, it was only logical that I should want to try my luck at the sport of kings. However, never having been to a horse race was sure to work against me in the betting department, unless I could devise some sort of system.

I bought a program, tout sheet, past records, and considerable other race information. There was no scientific method to approach this. I certainly was aware that I didn't know anything about horseflesh, so it would be impossible for me to look at a race horse and gauge his qualifications to run.

It was very late in the racing season. I hadn't been able to glean any surefire bets from my reading material. The odds didn't seem to tell me too much, and then it came to me: All the owners had several horses running at the track. Some of them had obviously had very poor racing seasons by now. They might have difficulty paying their feed and stall rentals. Wouldn't it be logical for the track to subtly encourage the big winners and the fast horses to have their jockeys just hold back a little bit? It seemed economically very sensible to let the non-winning stables win a few races.

Feverishly I studied the forms to find the stable numbers of the horses who had won the least over the season. Regardless of any other factors, this method should be the best chance for a neophyte horse race gambler like myself. I put two dollars on the nose of 112, which had the poorest record of any stable entered in the race. I may not know anything about horses, I reasoned, but I'm not stupid. The horses roared by to the finish line, and sure enough, the stable 112 representative won handily. I whooped with excitement and pounded my wife on the back. This was going to be easy. In the second race, it was 108 that needed to win some money desperately. Once again my two-dollar bet came home a winner.

Until about the fifth race I had won every time. The man sitting next to me was obviously a race track regular. He wore dark glasses and had on a long billed cap to further shade his eyes. Forms stuck out of every pocket of his sports jacket. He had been busily writing notes and figures and placing various complicated bets. I hadn't seen him win yet.

He leaned over toward me and in a hoarse whisper asked, "How you bettin' 'em, kid?"

I thought this guy looked as though he had been following horse racing for at least forty years. Surely he had hit upon my simple solution by now. I explained patiently that my method of using the non-winning stable numbers wouldn't work early in the year, but it was sure paying off now. He agreed.

"Where you gettin' them stable numbers?" he wanted to know.

"Right here on the racing form," I pointed out for him, wondering how he could have possibly missed that in all his years of betting.

"That's the weight the horse is carrying!" he said derisively and turned his back to me.

After learning this bit of information I dropped my

"system." I tried betting on the way the horse looked, going with the favorite, using the number of letters in the jockey's last name—anything! The results were always the same. I lost every remaining race.

I had taken a pretty good beating, too, when I traded the big, now extinct Nash, on the much smaller Rambler. Now that my horse race system was ruined, I couldn't even plan on making a big score to get some of my money back. Sometimes, you can know too much, or think you do, about cars as well as horses.

When I traded that troublesome '57 Nash for a much smaller 1961 Rambler four-door it looked like a very wise move. The Rambler automobile first came on the market in 1902 and was now a part of the new conglomerate, American Motors Company.

I stopped paying the huge horsepower feed bills on the Nash. My new car had an advanced aluminum engine that got excellent mileage. It had few amenities. No power steering or brakes, no air conditioning, no automatic transmission. Even the seats were spartan. In fact, in our only major concession to comfort, we had a local upholsterer add more foam padding to the factory seats. Of course, they did recline and make into a bed of sorts.

The little overhead-valve, six-cylinder engine had some pulling power. We had a fifteen-foot travel trailer that we hooked behind it for weekend trips or for the family's two-week vacation to the mountains of Colorado. It was on one of these sojourns that we learned a lot about pulling trailers. First of all, it really doesn't seem to make much difference in gas mileage whether a trailer is pulled with a 130-horsepower engine or a 300-horsepower monster. You can still figure on about eight to ten miles per gallon. The old big block engine probably didn't get more than about twelve MPG without the trailer, whereas the small engine would hit at least twenty-five on solo outings.

Why would one ever want to use a large engine for towing? The small one often had to be driven in second gear in headwinds and downshifted on every little hill. Looking in the rearview mirror while ascending the switchbacks of a mountain road in low gear at a wide-open fifteen miles an hour would reveal a long string of cars with irate drivers. Engine and transmission durability with the small engine may also be a problem.

We were traveling that year with Eddie, the Cadillac man, who had built a fold-down camping trailer. Although his trailer was heavy, it had no appreciable wind drag. The big Cadillac handled the trailer on the mountain roads fairly easily. For some unknown reason, we decided to pull both our trailers over a stretch of road known officially as the Trail Ridge Road in Rocky Mountain National Park. It's common name in Colorado is "the High Drive." It may still be the highest automobile pass in the world.

Once we got on that road, there was no way to turn around with the trailer attached. We knew before we had driven very far up the mountain that it was certainly going to test the merit of the Rambler. I shifted the manual transmission down from second gear, where I had been driving since the road began its ascent, into low. The speedometer indicated twenty-five miles per hour and falling. Surprisingly, once the vehicle reached about fifteen MPH, it just hung in there and pulled. The problem was, as we neared 12,000 feet, the low oxygen level at that altitude began to affect the gas mixture and reduce the engine power.

Just when I thought we had it made, with the high point of the pass being only a few hundred yards ahead, we ran into road construction. These high elevation mountain roads, although generally asphalt covered, tend to break up rapidly. That's what was going on here. We were stopped by a flagman on a gravel surface awaiting a new coat of "road tar." When the signal man waved us to proceed on through, I hit the gas and let out the clutch.

There was a spinning of wheels and a clattering of small

rocks into the wheel wells. The engine chugged, coughed, and died. I tried this procedure several times until it became obvious to everyone in the long line of traffic we were holding up that the car did not have the power to pull the trailer up that steep grade from a dead stop. The construction workers were beginning to get testy at this turn of events.

Fortunately, Eddie, who was following me with his Cadillac and trailer, had an idea. He found a three-foot piece of a two-by-four in his trunk. (Eddie always carried strange things in his trunk.)

"Here's what we're going to do," he proclaimed. "You give her all she's got and just keep it floor-boarded. I'm going to get up there by the right front wheel and each time she moves a little I'm going to keep that block behind the wheel to keep it from rolling back and killing the engine."

I was dubious, but there didn't appear to be any alternative. This was a rear-wheel drive car, so the front wheel Ed was going to block would not have engine power spinning it. I revved up the engine and let out the clutch. The car and trailer moved a few inches up the mountain as I kept the power on. With each move, Eddie pushed the block forward behind the tire, until after several feet the car was slowly pulling the load under its own power. At that point he simply jerked the board out of the way. We crept up over the top to the applause of the construction workers. To this day I still think I've got to be one of the few people to pull a full-size camping trailer over the High Drive with a little Rambler six.

Believe me, I'd never want to do it again.

It did prove to me that the Rambler had more pulling power than I ever thought possible. I even pulled boats with it and generally found it to be a highly dependable car.

My main complaint was that I had overreacted by buying a totally stripped-down model following all the trouble I had with the big, over-accessorized Nash. Furthermore, the Rambler was bright yellow. (Which would have been more appropriate for the '57 Nash.) It happened to be the only model of its kind in the showroom, and I was more than ready to buy any color just to get rid of the continuing expenses on the Nash.

Then I started to read automotive articles and listen to resident car experts.

"That aluminum engine will never stand up. If you ever get it hot, you'll warp the block and have to buy a whole new engine," friends and relatives advised me.

The car magazines were quick to point out that the aluminum engine had been tried in the past and proved to be a disaster in other cars. Being lightweight is its major advantage, while lack of durability is the killer, they said. One thing for certain, such comments had a lot to do with the demise of the Rambler engine. I had some 60,000 hard miles on mine in two years and decided it would be prudent to consider a trade. There was no indication of any trouble, no oil use or unusual noises, but—

So I went back to my favorite dealer. There had been a major styling and drive train change with the 1963 Rambler. Furthermore, American Motors has revived another well known name from the past, the Ambassador. Since this was a small car for its time, and since it shared its body style with the regular Rambler, the car became the Rambler Ambassador.

We struck the same deal as before, $2,000 and my car. For that I got a 327 V-8 and air conditioning. The 327 engine should not be confused with the same size engine made by Chevy. Most people just assumed that Rambler was using engines bought from Chevy, but that was not the case. This was a new in-house design, and a good one. The interior was quite plush, as befitted an Ambassador, but I bought a manual transmission with overdrive rather than the available automatic. Of course the car still had those reclining travel bed seats and the excellent heating and ventilation system designed by the old Nash motors.

Several years later, I was driving by a house out in the country when I spotted a yellow 1961 Rambler sitting in front of the garage. As I got closer I saw a small dent in a piece of chrome strip on the trunk. I had put that there myself while loading a boat and cramping the wheels of the car so short that the winch on the boat trailer dinged the chrome. No question, it was my old car.

Just about then a man came out the back door and headed toward the car. He looked familiar, but I didn't know his name. I couldn't restrain my curiosity. After the normal pleasantries I commented, "I used to own that Rambler of yours over there."

"Yup. Seen your name on the title." So he knew who I was.

"Given you any trouble?" I asked.

"Nope. Had to grind the valves a while back."

"And the aluminum engine, ever had any trouble with the block?"

"I didn't know it had an aluminum engine."

"Sure does. How many miles you got on her?"

"'Bout 220,000, more or less."

"*Two hundred and twenty thousand*?" I repeated in disbelief. "You've really put it over the road, haven't you?"

"Yup. Got a sister in California. Go out to see her three or four times a year. Do a lot of gadding around."

I told you there was such a thing as knowing too much about horses and cars. I was scared of the Rambler aluminum engine at 60,000 miles, and he had put another 160,000 on it and all the maintenance problems he ever had was to grind the valves.

As usual, this proved something to me that could best be illustrated by an experience from my childhood. Like most boys, the first summer job Dad arranged for me was mowing our yard. One day the skill level of my work was advanced considerably. A large truck arrived at our house and dumped a huge pile of dusty, foul smelling stuff in our yard. Dad wasn't far behind. "Here's what we've got to do," He said, grabbing me away from *The Radio Boys and the Giant Flood*, which

I was reading.

"We" turned out to be me. I was to scoop this stuff into a wheelbarrow, take it all around the yard, and then rake it out smoothly. Seemed simple enough. I didn't realize how big that pile really was. I don't think Dad did either, for when he came home at lunch, I had finished most of the front yard and there was still a huge amount left.

"You're going to have to put it on thicker," he told me. "This sheep dung is great stuff and our yard really needs some help." Dad was always a great believer in the theory that if a lot was good, a lot more was even better.

At least I knew for sure what that odiferous stuff was now. I dutifully went on about my application job until Dad got home late that afternoon.

"I see you've got it done," Dad said, as I was raking the last of the inch-thick fertilizer among the few tops of the blades of grass still protruding. "Now we've got to water the thunder out of it and soak it in."

I did. Then Dad watered some more. By the end of the next day, the green sprouts of grass were turning yellow, and the next day brown. Look on the bright side, I thought. The yard may look a lot worse, but it sure stinks to high heaven. I reminded Dad of that.

"Don't worry," he said, "It always looks like its dying before it comes back strong." He was forever the optimist. After another week of more heavy watering, the "lawn" had turned to mud and sheepshit. Dad bought innumerable bags of grass seed over the next couple years, but none of it could live through what we had done to that ground. It had just started to recover a little bit on its own when Dad sold the house and we moved.

Now, I should tell you that I've told that story, and the one about my yellow Rambler, to my friend, Coady. Coady claims to be a relative of Buffalo Bill Cody. He says the famous showman never could spell his last name so he just started leaving the "a" out of it.

Today Coady is a gregarious and aggressive businessman. He's the sort of guy who draws people to him like gnats go after perfume. But it wasn't always like that. Judging by some of his yarns, life on the farm with his parents was pretty tame, until another one of Coady's shenanigans created a furor. He and I often swapped down-home experiences.

"You're always telling me about the trouble you got into when your dad got you into some kind of work," he said. "Now I'll tell you one like that you can't top.

"I loved the farm," he said, "The outdoors, the freedom, the river bottom, the fresh air, wild-rose smells, and the horses, all those things you reminisce about when you think back to life on a small farm," Coady said.

"But let me tell you, when you throw in the field work, riding a slow moving tractor up and down those endless rows with nothing much to do, you remember that most of the time farming is pretty dull."

"Yeh, Coady, I can see where a guy like you could get pretty bored."

"Actually, I'm easily satisfied. If I just could have read a good book at the same time, it wouldn't have been so bad. Dad's tractor didn't require much attention when I was discing, but it did take just enough to foul up anything else I might want to do. Dad had told me a couple weeks before to get out there on the weekend, when I wasn't in school, and disc that south field, but I kept finding things I would rather do."

"So you're saying you didn't pay much attention to what your father asked you to do?" I continued pushing him toward his point. I was anxious to hear the end of this story.

"Are you serious? I always did exactly what Dad told me to do. Just not always when he told me to do it," he smiled. "My Dad knew I was never going to make it as a farmer. He also knew that I hated driving a tractor," he continued. "Dad bought this brand-new John Deere, not the fancy kind you see today with an air conditioned cab and stereo, but a pretty decent tractor for the times. Dad was really proud of it."

''And he let you drive it?''

''Not exactly let me. He wasn't too happy with my work performance right then. Or school either, for that matter. Dad was pretty busy with spring work and told me I had to get that river ground worked right then or he was going to whale the tar out of me. I was in high school at the time and, although I was probably stronger and quicker than he was, I was still plenty scared of him,'' he admitted.

''Actually, there was a certain kick in driving that brand-new, powerful machine and feeling it churn up the earth behind me. That feeling lasted about fifteen minutes. Then it was off into zombie land for me.'' he mused.

''It was a beautiful, warm spring day, bright sunshine, several million things I would rather be doing. I took my shirt off to catch a little sun and was half-dozing my way along. Suddenly there was a little dust kicking up off the gravel road coming toward me, right next to where I was working along the fence-line. It turned out to be this good-looking neighbor girl in a red convertible driving along very slowly. From my high vantage point in the tractor seat I could see she was wearing the shortest pair of short-shorts and the skimpiest halter top I had ever seen.'' Coady paused and licked his lips.

''And you stopped and spent the rest of the day with her, and didn't get the field work done,'' I surmised.

''Not exactly,'' he said. ''She waved. I waved back. She had that car just creeping along the road. I don't know what she was looking at, but I sure know what I was. I turned around in the seat and watched her drive every foot of that road off behind me.''

''It was too late when I realized that I had come to the end of our field. By the time I could get the tractor stopped, it had ripped through a barbed wire fence and into a grove of trees along the river. All the crashing and breaking of tree limbs with Dad's new tractor was pretty horrifying.''

''What'd you do?'' I asked expectantly.

''Well, I knew Dad would be mad as hops when he found

out what had happened. I climbed down off the tractor and looked over the damage. Some scratches in the new paint from the barbed wire, the exhaust stack was knocked off the top of the engine, but not as bad as I thought it might be,'' he laughed.

''Problem was, this was certain to put an end to my social calendar, and I kind of thought that I might want to get better acquainted with that neighbor girl in the convertible.''

''Did you?'' I asked.

''First things first. I walked over to the old pickup and headed for town. At the John Deere dealer I bought some green touch-up paint and went back to the scene of the disaster. I sprayed it on the front where the barbed wire had scratched it, and actually I didn't think it looked half bad. The stack, where it had hit a tree was something else again. I found that I could fasten the pipe back upright, and there was just this one small dent in it. But the round top was crunched-up beyond repair.'' Coady continued.

''Then fate entered the picture. Lying very close to my feet there in the underbrush was an old rusty coffee can, almost the exact size of the mangled stack top. I got a few tools out of the box on the tractor, punched a couple holes in the sides of the can near the bottom, put the metal screws back in it and fastened it to the exhaust pipe. Didn't look too bad. I spray-painted that sucker with the John Deere green paint and backed out of the trees. I let the paint dry for a few minutes while I fixed the fence, and then went back to a really intense job of discing that field.''

''Did your Dad ever find out?'' I asked in anticipation.

''Well, it was almost dark when I finished with the field. I knew Dad would probably check on things before he turned in, but with a little luck, he'd probably never even notice my neat repair job on the tractor. I had pulled the John Deere off facing the trees, and a pretty good walk from the road.''

''But you knew he'd find it sooner or later,'' I interjected.

''I figured Dad would be too busy seeing if I had screwed

up the discing job to go over there to check on it. Then if a few days went by before he used the tractor again, the new would be kind of worn off and maybe he wouldn't get too excited about my repairs. Besides, it was Saturday night and if I was going to get grounded, I sure didn't want it to be that night,'' he grinned.

''I went on home for supper, but Dad hadn't gotten in yet. About the time I finished eating, he walked in the door.'' Coady paused and looked at me, knowing I would empathize with him.

''I could tell by his scowl there was bad news ahead,'' Coady said. ''When he called me by my real name, I knew that was all she wrote.''

''Lenny, whut-in-the-damned-hell did you do to my new tractor?'' he demanded.

''Dad was not very experienced at cursing. It was all downhill from that point. I didn't get to go to town that night, or even get a chance make time with the neighbor girl that whole next summer. I never did have guts enough to tell Dad the whole story.'' He sat back with a great look of satisfaction.

''I hate to tell you this, Coady, but I didn't finish my fertilizer story,''' I told him.

''I mighta known it,'' he sighed.

''Dad got me a job as the official caretaker of a an enormous lawn surrounding a home on a huge corner lot. Dad assured the people that I had had considerable experience applying fertilizer. He managed to omit the result it had on our yard. This lawn was a beautiful green carpet that grew like crazy. About twice a week I was over at this fancy house pushing the clattering, hand-powered mower. Then the lady of the house told me it was time to fertilize.

''Frankly, I couldn't imagine why, as lush and rapid growing as that lawn was. When I returned on the appointed fertilizer application day, there was a pickup truck full of something smelly sitting by the sidewalk. 'We're going to be out of town for a few days,' she told me. 'Just be sure you water real good twice a day, after you put it on.' I assured her I would.

"A surprise awaited me in the truck. Cow cakes. These were dried and hard. How could I break them up? I tried with a rake and a hoe without much success. They didn't granulate like the sheep dung had. They came apart in fairly large pieces. Also, to my horror, I discovered there was no wheelbarrow to move the stuff out of the old pickup and around the big yard. No keys in the truck. I didn't know how to drive anyway, but I would have tried.

"This meant that I had to take a shovel full of cow manure, walk to the farthest point in the yard, spread it around, and walk back to the truck. This took a great deal of time. I worked on it for almost two days before I got around to trying to rake it in and pulverize the pieces. I couldn't water it yet, of course, or I would have had an unbelievable gooey mess to walk through. When I turned over the first of the larger pieces, that beautiful green grass underneath was a putrid yellow."

Coady stared at me incredulously.

"I raked feverishly. More pieces broken up, more yellow spots. It looked as though the lawn had some sort of off-color chicken pox. I finished as quickly as possible and began a day-long saga of watering from every possible hydrant, flooding the yard where I couldn't spray it. Brown water was soon flooding over the curb and into the street. Observant neighbors were giving me stern looks and turning up their noses.

"The next day the owners arrived home. I was wearing my five-buckle overshoes and still watering. They looked in horror at the yard. I didn't wait to be fired. I simply climbed on my bicycle and rode off into the sunset, my days as a yard boy completed."

"OK," Coady said, "You always use those boyhood stories to illustrate a point. What's this one?"

"What I learned applies to all the people who give me so much bad advice," I smiled at him. "In this case it was how that aluminum engine in that Rambler would never hold up.

If you're going to lay it on thick, you had better be darn sure you've got it right. Otherwise, you could end up with everyone knowing you're just one of the sheep who are busily following each other and producing the stuff I had to spread on our yard."

"I give up," Coady groaned. But he really didn't.

# 9

## *Surefire Investments*

YOU PROBABLY ALREADY KNOW IT, but it never hurts to point out that cars are not investments in the same sense that stock in a car company is. Even a stock investment is easier to understand in the perspective of the past. If you had been given a chance in the earlier part of this century to buy stock in one of two companies, which would you have chosen at the time?

1. The booming Stutz Company of America, riding the crest of popularity with their Stutz Bearcat models.

2. Financially troubled General Motors Corporation, and their stable of sedate cars, completely lacking in imaginative engineering.

Sure, with hindsight you wouldn't consider the now-bankrupt Stutz company, but do you think you would have had the foresight to have purchased stock in an out-of-favor GM? Most of us wouldn't have.

While we know too well about the losses, people have also made huge amounts of money on certain cars. For instance, look at the owners of Duesenbergs. These cars are often sold today at pricey car auctions for a couple million each. The problem is, Duesenbergs were out of the price range of most people when they were originally sold new.

With any model you may choose to keep as an investment you also run the risk of storing one of these babies for fifty years or more, and maintaining it in mint condition, only to find that you have kept the wrong model. No huge bucks profit. Or, on the darker side, you may have died during the long term it takes in most cases to realize substantial gains on automobiles.

Collector cars are a step below the true antiques and mint condition models, which have often been restored. Most have considerable value over their original purchase price. The problem here is that their owners also have put considerably more money in them than their initial cost. These cars are a labor of love, and reflect a pride in ownership and personal accomplishment. None of those things can be measured as a return on an investment. True, you might luck out and pick the right stock, or even the right car to hold onto. But in truth it's more of a rich man's game than one for most of us.

However, my own investments point out the fact that all of us try to make money when we can. This bizarre group of blunders should be filed under "Financial Disasters." You already know some of my investments directly relating to cars. These don't necessarily fall into the car category, but may give you an insight into what motivates some investments that turn into something else altogether.

My neighbor, Chris, was a gambler at heart. He bought penny stocks, a notoriously speculative stock investment overall, played the horses and just about anything else that involved the thrill of a possible quick profit. He was interesting to be around, and you were sure to learn something, since he was a keen observer of all things financial.

One day in the late 1970s Chris asked me if I knew why the government was selling silver mint sets far below the cost of silver.

"I thought they stopped selling them last year," I said.

"So did I,' he said, "but I was reading some U.S. Mint production and sales figures in a financial newspaper, and it showed some limited sales this year. Looks to me like a guy could make some big bucks buying from the government below market value and reselling on the open market."

"I can't believe they would do anything that stupid," I replied.

"I think I'm going to buy some of those sets," Chris said.

Later, I thought about Chris's statement. He was usually right on something like that, so I called the Mint. Yes, after a brief closedown, they were selling the silver issue sets again, and no, there was no limit. I couldn't believe it. I immediately ordered a large number of the sets, sold them the same day they were received, and doubled my money.

I went over to see Chris. "Say, I'd sure like to thank you for putting me onto that silver deal with the government," I said.

"Yeah. I see they've closed ordering again now."

"How many did you buy?" I queried.

"Uh, I didn't, uh, order any," he admitted hesitantly. Chris really wasn't interested in sure things, anymore than he would have considered betting on a favorite at the race track.

This investment must be considered in the context of what I did with the profits. I decided that since that deal worked out so well, I'd better keep my eyes and ears open for more of these inside opportunities. My wife and I were eating breakfast in a rather plush hotel in Omaha. A man sat down at a table crowded in next to us, and we started a conversation.

It seems he had been attending a chef's school in New York City and had made an overnight stop to visit with one of Omaha's self made millionaire restauranteurs. I immediately recognized the name. Perhaps, I thought, I should learn more about this.

"You're going to be a chef?" I asked.

"Oh no, I'm already a chef with a major West Coast food chain. They sent me to school just so I could select the most promising of the graduates, and work with them during classes. You can pretty well tell the few who will turn out to be the really good chefs."

That was obviously an interesting premise. "And these chefs, are they going to work for your organization?"

"Not directly," he said, "We're developing a spinoff company. They'll be employed by the new company. It's just been listed on the stock market, by the way. That's why I stopped here last night. Willie is one of the principal stockholders and he wanted a personal progress report."

"Any other names involved I might be familiar with?" I asked.

"Just that one is from around here, so you might not know the rest. You'd sure know the companies they run though." He listed several large franchises and soft drink concerns and the people who had taken them to great success.

"That's a pretty high-powered bunch," I observed.

"They're confident, and our company is confident. We think we've got the organizational plan to get this thing booming. Getting top-notch people to run the food preparation is the real key. We think we have that under control."

"What did you say the name of the new company is?"

"Flakey Jakes," he said.

When I got home, my first phone call was to a stockbroker I knew. "What do you know about a company named Flakey Jakes?"I asked.

"Flakey Jakes? Never heard of it."

"Can you check it out for me right away?" I told him who was involved in the management and board of directors, and why I was interested.

"Sure. Get back to you shortly."

When the phone rang I grabbed it on the first ring. "You may be onto something hot," the broker said. "Everything you told me about who's involved checks out. There hasn't been a big run up on it yet, so I ordered a chunk of shares for myself.''

''Thanks, I'll get back to you later,'' I said prudently.

I called Chris, the man who put me onto the silver deal, and provided him with the information on Flakey Jakes.

''Would you do me a favor and call a couple of the brokers you deal with and see what you can find out?''

Chris knew a lot more of these financial wizards than I did. He reported back a couple hours later.

''They all agree this is a very hot deal,'' he said. ''I bought 500 shares.''

I remembered that Chris had passed up the deal with the silver, so this must really be inside stuff. I called my broker back and immediately bought 500 shares too, using about half my mint set profit.

Flakey Jakes soon jumped a dollar a share. Then it rose another fifty cents and appeared to be poised for a rocket ascent. Meanwhile, Chris had told a couple of his cronies about it, and they had gotten in at the slightly higher levels.

Then suddenly, Flakey Jakes lost its initial gains. My broker said he thought it was a temporary correction. The stock lost another dollar, then cut in half in one day, and half again the next.

''What happening?'' I demanded from my broker.

''I don't know, but I don't like it. My company was making a market in that stock, but not any more. I think we should sell it.''

It didn't seem reasonable to me that a company with all that industry clout, expertise, and financial backing could possibly go under that quickly. I decided to hold on. Chris bought some more shares at the new low costs to maximize his profits when it rebounded. I considered his suggestion, but decided against it. Within another six months Flakey Jakes was down the tubes.

My good friend, Harold, was always getting into get rich quick deals. He had a world of ability and charisma running out his ears. The problem was that he was convinced he could make the big score without really working for it or inheriting it. It's the American Dream of course, and some people achieve it. Not Harold. He had the brains, but greed often would overcome his judgment, making his timing terrible.

I remember years ago he asked me if I wanted to go into the cattle business with him. President Nixon had imposed a wage and price freeze in an attempt to slow down inflation. The freeze was to be lifted September 4 of that year.

"I've lined up a big herd of cattle out in Western Nebraska," he told me. "Everybody knows what's going to happen to the price of cattle after the freeze comes off. The price is going through the roof. You can get in for $25,000."

"What kind of winter provisions have you got lined up to feed them in case the price doesn't go up right away?" I asked.

"What do you mean,'doesn't go up'? Everybody knows that cattle are going sky high! I'm not going to feed 'em, I'm going to sell 'em! My neighbor thinks it's such a good deal he bought two shares at $25,000 apiece."

"But if everybody knows the price of beef it going up, why is the rancher anxious to sell in the first place?" I wondered.

"He's a friend of mine," Harold assured me.

"Sounds just too speculative for my tastes, " I told him, "but I hope it goes for you." I really meant that. Of course, the cattle prices plummeted that September and Harold ended up selling frozen western Nebraska beef door to door. It was probably an excellent deal for beef buyers, but not for Harold.

During the OPEC oil scare of the 1970s Harold devised another rather complicated way of getting in on the action. He formed a company in Oklahoma with his brother-in-law that dealt in the large scale leasing of oil lands. Harold saw the opulent life-styles of these people and believed wealth was there for the taking. He bought an airplane and commuted from Nebraska to Tulsa in a style befitting a new oil tycoon.

The problem was that the oil patch had started to go sour.

Harold was not alone is misreading this, but with oil suddenly plentiful again, the interest in new leases waned. His almost-high-flying company got shot down before it had a chance to soar.

Harold's incredibly bad timing on these ventures was becoming noticeable. For a while I really didn't want to spend much time around him for fear that I might in some way be jinxing his ventures by not participating in them. I hadn't seen him for a couple years when one day I decided to stop by and check out what was sure to be another new get-rich-quick deal.

We had a brief reunion, interrupted by constantly ringing phones. I gathered from the conversations that Harold was involved in buying coins and precious metals.

"I don't care if you have to mortgage your home, your car, and sell your wife," he laughed as he told me how simple it was. "Now is the time to get all your cash in silver. It's going to $100 an ounce, just as sure as we're sitting here."

The numerous phone callers were getting roughly the same message, without the histrionics. These were the investors in Harold's new Precious Metals Investments, Inc. Harold was busily buying silver on other phone lines, while recruiting more capital to buy new hoards of the metal.

"What do you do with all this silver once you buy it?" I asked innocently.

"Sell it to a fabricator down in Georgia for a tidy profit. Beauty of it is that he pays me when its processed, not on receipt. That way, as the silver prices go up, I make even more just while its waiting for fabrication," he smiled happily.

"But that could work the other way, couldn't it?" I suggested.

"Are you serious? Silver is only $50 an ounce now, and everybody knows it's going to double," Harold said. "Sure you don't want to get in on it? I'm going to make my fortune and retire."

I begged off and began the eighty-mile drive home. That

gave me time to further reflect on the situation. Harold could be right, but what were the odds? As soon as I got home I told my wife, "Honey, remember the other half of those government silver mint sets and all those other old silver coins we took out of circulation and put in the bank box? Let's get them all together and sell them tomorrow."

"What made you think of that?"

"Let's just call it the Harold Principle," I told her.

What nobody knew was that the Hunt brothers had attempted to corner the entire market in the precious metal, billions of dollars worth. This had driven prices sky-high, and now the Hunt's silver empire was about to fall apart.

Sometimes it's better to be lucky than smart. We missed the century's highest silver price by a couple bucks an ounce, but the slide in price that followed eliminated Harold's company, and most other silver speculators as well.

Then there was the financial deal that proves another maxim: "If it sounds so absolutely ridiculous nobody would buy it, somebody probably will."

Four of us were sitting drinking coffee following a church meeting we had attended with friends in another town. My cousin Milo, a friend Bob, and Rupert, a church elder, had already discussed, and solved, most of the world's problems. At that point Rupert held forth on a new business venture for which he was accumulating capital.

Rupert is a very nice, well-meaning man. Unfortunately, he is a bit like Harold, only not so much in bad timing and luck as in gullibility. Rupert is a true believer. As far as he is concerned, everyone is totally honest. No matter how many times he gets taken, or his own inventions are misappropriated by someone else, Rupert is always back for one more try. His latest involvement was even more creative than most.

"You guys know old Herman, the water well witcher from over by Arcadia?" he asked.

Even I, a visitor from out of town, had heard of the legendary Herman. He was a little, stooped-shouldered man in a pair of dirty overalls. His age seemed to be undetermined, but certainly in his late eighties. Herman had "the gift." Farmers in the area would not even consider drilling a water well without first getting Herman to "witch" it. Most of them usually got a geology report and the advice of well drillers, but they still called in Herman to determine exact location of the proposed well.

Herman would select a forked willow stick or some other wood as long as it was fresh-cut and green. Then he would walk along the generally preferred area holding the stick by its forks in both hands. When the stick began to quiver and the suddenly pointed at the ground, that was the spot to drill the water well. I'm not here to tell you that witching for water is a scientific practice. I will tell you that Herman was almost always successful. This may have been because the world's largest underground aquifer lies below the hills and flatlands of Nebraska.

"Herman has discovered a secret that's going to make us all rich." Rupert confided. "He has found that he can use a welded, T-shaped piece of metal and witch for oil!"

There was laughter all around. "What's that metal rod doing?" Bob asked. "Pointing out cans of 10W-30 motor oil in his garage?" We all knew oil had never been discovered in this part of the country, despite repeated drilling operations.

"He's not doing it *here*," Rupert continued, undaunted by our obvious skepticism. "My partners and I are buying up oil lease land in Kentucky, in an area where oil has never been discovered, but near some really big oil operations."

"Who did you rope in this time?" cousin Milo laughed. "What makes you think Herman can witch for oil?"

Rupert looked around secretively and in a low voice said, "We rented a plane and used charts some of my partners had made up. We had Herman use his metal rod from the airplane. Every time we flew over an existing, producing oil field, that rod would witch it out and vibrate almost out of Herman's hands!"

The other three of us looked at each other, speechless. Did Rupert really believe this stuff?

"Then we flew over our leased land where everybody says there's no oil, and Herman witched out several huge veins of it again, just like he had over the producing wells." Rupert looked at us to see how we would react to this "proof."

I couldn't hold it back any longer. "What did you do then, Rupert, paint a white X on the floor of the airplane so you could be sure to find the place again?" Everybody laughed.

Rupert continued very seriously. "We've just about got all the capital we need to start drilling. Couple of twins, businessmen from Aurora, got in on the ground floor of this deal and put in a quarter of a million." Those were magic words in our part of the country, "get in on the ground floor."

"We're selling partnership interests at just $20,000 each. You boys interested?"

We winked at each other. Probably a real good deal, but not the kind of investment we're interested in, we agreed. Imagine my surprise when Rupert called me the next morning after I had arrived back home.

"Changed your mind on investing in our oil business?" Rupert asked. "It's a sure thing." That was another one of those cliches that seemed to get everybody around here excited.

Frankly, I thought it was a pretty gutsy call after all the kidding we had given him. Perhaps I had the word "sucker" stenciled on my forehead and didn't know it. But as I said, Rupert's a nice guy, even if he is excessively naive. "No thanks," I said politely.

"Since your cousin Milo just bought in, I thought maybe you had changed your mind." I almost swallowed the phone.

"I haven't got that kind of money for speculation," I said truthfully, realizing that Rupert was certain to be telling me the straight story about cousin Milo's investment. Rupert was no liar.

I excused myself from the phone for a suddenly important business engagement I had just created. Cousin Milo? The conservative who says he would just as soon throw his money away in Las Vegas as put it in the stock market? I couldn't get over it.

Of course, all the "oil investment" money soon disappeared, including Cousin Milo's and the money Rupert had gotten by mortgaging his home. The high rolling twins no longer had a phone listing and presumably moved on to visit greener pastures. The well witcher? I don't know how the twins managed to plant the oil witching idea in old Herman's mind. Nevertheless, they paid him well for his witching expertise, and gave the octogenarian an exciting airplane ride. He was the only one involved with the venture, besides the twin con artists, who made money on the deal. He didn't have any money to invest.

That's the way I am with some of the car investments I've seen. Remember the Tucker? It was based on a 1948 Oldsmobile that looked as though it had spent too much time in a custom body shop. A couple of features were very intriguing however. The car had a headlight directly in the center of its pointed hood. When you turned the steering wheel the light turned also to illuminate corners. It was said to have front-wheel drive and a highly fuel efficient, yet powerful, engine.

I saw one as it was being taken across the country on a drive to raise funds in the form of a stock issue in the Tucker company. Fortunately, like Herman the well-witcher, I didn't have any money either, or I probably would have purchased both the stock and the car.

Recently television and magazines have given considerable play to a new Jaguar being built in England by that company, which is now owned by Ford motors. It is a sports car capable of speeds over 200 miles per hour. The sleek machine is a looker. Its initial subscription of some 300 was sold out almost immediately at $300,000 each. Only prototypes had been built at that time, and it was anticipated to take about a year to complete the initial orders.

The largest percentage of buyers are from Belgium, a country which recently enacted a 50 MPH maximum speed limit Am I missing something here? This is supposed to be a road car, not something that will be driven on a race track. Or are all these people buying the new Jag to store away for investment?

Perhaps these people feel like my friend Coady does about speeding tickets.

"You had just as well have a neon sign on the trunk that says, 'Arrest me!' as drive that flashy red Corvette of yours one mile an hour over the speed limit," I observed. "Yeh, if they catch me," he said wryly.

"But you've told me about some horrendous speeding tickets you've had to pay," I reminded him. In his work Coady is always in a huge hurry to get somewhere.

"It's all in how you look at it," he said, "I consider it like a toll road. The speeding tickets are just the cost of driving on the highway." Coady did finally have a change of heart however. He sold the Corvette and bought an airplane.

At least the people who buy the 200MPH Jaguar have a company with a solid reputation behind them, regardless of whether the car turns out to be one of the true investment models. You may remember another ill-fated sports car, the DeLorean. This car rivaled the Tucker for a lack of funding. However, the former American big-three car company manager, John DeLorean, somehow managed to con the British government into building a manufacturing plant for the DeLorean and agreeing to support his pet project, within certain limits. He soon surpassed those limits and sped into bankruptcy.

The car design sounded great. The gull-winged doors had the entire sides of the car lifting up, being hinged into the roof and operated by hydraulics. Although not new in design, this solved one eternal complaint of sports car owners about how hard their cars are to get into.

The second innovation was an entire body made of stainless

steel. It was strong and offered years of rust-free service. The DeLorean design made sense to many of us. Luckily I didn't have the money to buy that one either.

The problem was that this heavy car lacked the promised sports car performance and handling proclaimed by its developer. It was fuel hungry, with an engine a couple of generations behind the top power plants of other new sports car designs. Although the DeLorean died an unhappy death, it is still possible that people who bought the car, like the Tucker and others before it, may have the last laugh. These are the rare cars that become museum pieces and collectors items.

The Jaguar sports car's eventual value? Who knows? If it is highly successful it could do great things for company profits. In that case its owners might have a hard time selling the car for anywhere near the $300,000 price tag at some future date. If it turns out to be a one-year unproductive venture for the manufacturer, it could be the buyers of the cars who ultimately make some really big bucks. If the Jag simply limps along with a few years of low sales, but enough to meet future collector demands, the chances are neither the manufacturer nor the car buyer will have made a wise investment.

That's the way it is with cars. If you buy them for investment, the risks are very high. If you buy them for transportation and perhaps a certain amount of prestige, like most of us do, you're almost guaranteed to lose money.

What kind of deal is that? Well, at least we don't lose as much money as the would-be investors. Then to, we get to drive our cars instead of having them set on blocks somewhere in eternal storage while waiting for the unlikely big score.

# 10

## *Darting into the Fray*

"DO YOU KNOW THE DIFFERENCE between a war horse and a dray horse?" old timers used to ask me.

"A war horse darts into the fray." Haw, haw! And now it seemed that once more I was about to dart into the fray of car trading.

"Pete," I said one day, after about two years of ownership of my '63 Rambler Ambassador, "Make me a deal on a new one."

"Depends on what you want on it" he said.

"The wife wants an automatic transmission," I lied. I wanted it, but automatics were supposed to be made for women. Ardelle always liked whatever car we presently owned and was balky about trading. Pete had it easy. I had to sell my wife.

"Probably about $2,000 to boot," he said. "How's the windshield?" This was a ritual question with car dealers in our area at the time, since many of our non-highway connecting roads were still gravel surface, presenting a death threat to windshields.

"Well, look at it," I said. "Don't see any holes or anything do you?" He grunted his salesman's grunt.

"How many miles you got on those tires?"

"Probably 10,000, I don't know, we could check the records. They got half their wear left in them," I said, optimistically.

One of the main reasons I was interested in the 1965 Ambassador was that disc brakes were available as an option. I had read that discs were far superior to the drum brakes that were common on almost all American cars at the time.

"I'd want the disc brakes, too," I told him.

"Keep adding stuff on and the price goes up," he observed.

"That's OK. If I don't like your price, I'll just have to look somewhere else," I grinned at him.

There was some controversy over disc brakes at the time. A newspaper reporter had asked a General Motors engineer why tiny American Motors was introducing discs as an option while other American makes were not. The engineer said that his company felt that discs were only marginally better than drum brakes, and then only in certain conditions. Furthermore, he told the writer, the American consumer would never pay the extra money for any so-called safety feature. Therefore, GM cars would never have disc brakes as far as he was concerned.

The Europeans, however, had already proved disc brakes were superior. Only American Motors, among U.S. companies had followed the lead. The big three had been burned on technology too many times before. Styling and horsepower were the proven sales winners. It was another three years before disc brakes were optional on most GM makes, as they and other car makers followed American Motors lead in the U.S. market. American Motors was then near the peak of its popularity. This engineering coup was another shot in the

arm for the company.

I'm reminded of our cousin KoAnn's son Dana who was just learning to print short sentences in grade school. Each day the teacher was having students write a sentence that best described their father, then their mother, then brothers and sisters, and so on. Dana had apparently been quite impressed with the lack of hair on his father's head. A very popular slogan at the time among men who lacked scalp hair was, "Bald is beautiful."

At the next parent-teacher conference, Dana's teacher told KoAnn she thought she would certainly enjoy seeing the sentence her son had written describing his father. Dana had carefully printed, "BALLED IS BEAUTIFUL."

The moral here is that it doesn't take much of a change to make a huge difference in the end result. Disc brakes as opposed to drum brakes mean stopping from fifty to eighty feet sooner in a car driving sixty miles an hour. If the road is wet, disc brakes don't fade. When driving in mountainous terrain, there is much less danger of brakes getting extremely hot from overuse, causing a total lack of braking power. Safety was a greater factor among buyers than expected by most automobile companies, and American Motors had guessed correctly for a change.

On the other hand, there can be safety and personal injury problems with any mode of transportation, even with the two-wheeled people-powered variety. Not long after our daughter Dawn had gotten her first new bicycle, I was out in the driveway washing the car. I hadn't seen her coming, but there she was, bedraggled, and pulling along a bicycle whose front wheel would obviously no longer turn.

"What happened to your new bike?" I asked. She dabbed at the corner of her eye.

"Are you hurt?" I could see her pride certainly was.

"Un-huh."

Her knees were suspiciously dirty, but she seemed to be otherwise OK. The bicycle' frame, on the other hand, was cracked in two places, and the wheel was folded back to the pedals.

"Want to tell me what happened?"

"I hit a little bump in the street," she said evasively.

"Don't worry, honey," I told her. "I think my friend at the auto body shop can weld that frame, paint it, replace the wheel and your bike will be good as new."

She brightened a little bit.

"Want to tell Daddy how it happened?"I asked again.

"I *know*, but I don't want to talk about it," she frowned.

When I got inside to tell my wife about the bike accident, the phone was ringing. It was a neighbor from a block over.

"Is Dawn all right?" she asked, "She was riding along

without holding on to the handle bars, just looking around real proud of herself, and she crashed right into the back of our car.''

''She's fine. Do any damage to the car?'' I asked half-seriously.

''No, you can't hurt that old tank. When I saw her dragging away that bike she was already half way down the block, so I couldn't catch her to see if she was all right.''

The mystery of the little ''bump'' in the road was solved.

My father used a bicycle to get back and forth to work before he could afford a car. One morning the circus came to town. Any self-respecting circus had a colorful steam calliope. A few musical notes on that in the early morning and people would turn out to watch the circus unload, and buy tickets for the performances later that day.

Dad was pedaling alongside the calliope and watching it with great interest, when he crashed into the back of a slow moving car. Fortunately, like Dawn, he wasn't hurt, but the bike suffered a much worse fate.

Regardless, in 1965 disc brakes were a rarity on American cars. I wanted them. That willingness to pick up on improved engineering was among the reasons the *Popular Mechanics* owners' survey showed Rambler leading all other makes in number of owners who said they would buy the car again. That was true throughout the decade of the 1960s.

However, all that may prove is that the General Motors engineer who dragged his feet on disc brakes may have been correct. Not from an engineering standpoint, but from a company survivability one. History has shown that, usually, the American carmaker with the most advanced engineering has been the company first to fail.

Since 1930 more than thirty makes of American cars have gone out of business. There were many different makes of cars prior to that time, but often those companies were tiny enterprises eliminated by normal attrition or mergers. Often an innovation that caused a company's failure was adopted throughout the industry within five years of its introduction and eventually gained public acceptance.

As a boy I remember watching our neighbor, Mrs. Applegate, drive sedately down the street in her 1912 Baker Electric. I was fascinated by the vehicle. I would often run along on the sidewalk, just feet away from this silent machine, as it made its way down the street. It wasn't hard for me to keep up, as the cruising speed must have been about six or eight miles an hour.

Mrs. Applegate once showed me the immaculate interior of the Baker. It was much like an old, ornate stagecoach. There was a tiller-like device rather than a conventional steering wheel. This resembled a long rod with a fancy handle on the end, coming across the vehicle from the left side, horizontally across the lap of the driver. The quilted seats were as luxurious as the parlor davenport at home. Mrs. Applegate was making no drastic change in going from her living room to her transportation. The car looked similar from either front or rear.

General Electric had funded the Baker Electric when it came on the market in 1898. Women loved the cars for their silence. They were impressed that many horrible things, like the crank and spark advance weren't even in the cars, nor were many of the other devices that often went wrong on gasoline-powered vehicles.

Many drivers had a tendency to "ride the clutch" with the noisy internal combustion engine, and that engine required a gear-shifting arrangement. Apparently, keeping one foot rested lightly on the clutch pedal was thought to give the driver quicker access to fully depressing the clutch, which was necessary for a complete stop. However, when the foot was held even very gently on the clutch while driving, the clutch plates were only partially engaged. Abnormal wear resulted.

To get moving if you held your foot lightly on the clutch pedal, there would be a great roaring of the engine with several times more power required than would normally be needed.

The radiator fan blades would sound like an airplane propeller. The result of this was the taunting shouts of small boys. "Let out the clutch, Gramps! The fan will never pull her!" This taunting upset female drivers considerably more than it did their male counterparts, maybe because there were relatively few women drivers, and they were very sensitive of their status.

Additional noise was certainly unwanted. With the Baker Electric this never occurred. There was no clutch, no engine, and no fan. There was only an electric motor and blessed silence. By eliminating many of the parts needed with the gasoline engine, the Baker had only one thing to go wrong with it. It always did: the battery. There wasn't enough capacity to power the car for long drives, even at very low speeds. The batteries frequently went bad and required expensive replacement.

There have been similar problems with every electric car that has been built to date. Imagine: Nearly a century has gone by with only minimal progress on electric-powered cars. No pollution, virtually silent running, no smelly, inflammable, gasoline to deal with—and no solution to the storage battery problem.

Other alternate fuel sources are under development or in limited use at present. These include liquid natural gas and propane, which are in much greater supply in the United States than oil. With these fuels, larger and heavier storage tanks, lower mileage, and less power are problems in present state-of-the-art vehicle testing.

Other fuels are made from coal or other fossil fuels, plus methanol from wood. All of the fuel sources discussed thus far have the same disadvantage as oil. They are a finite resource or have very slow regrowth. We do, however, have within the United States a great deal more of these natural resources. An estimated 300-year supply of coal, for example. However, if we begin turning these resources into automobile fuel, that length of time would be cut drastically.

Also, there are serious environmental considerations in the form of pollution associated with the production and distribution of any of these fuels.

Sometimes, it seems that none of the choices we face is a good one. Years ago I was traveling with my parents on a vacation trip to California in Dad's 1929 Pontiac. This was quite a feat in those days, both financially and from the fact that this nine-year-old car wasn't in very good shape. In order to make the trip possible, Dad had agreed to take an older couple along with us who would buy all the gas. They wanted to see a son who had moved west several years before.

We had few troubles with the vehicle as we motored along at a steady forty-miles-per-hour. I slept through all of southern Wyoming. I remember my mother became quite upset with me when she was trying to point out several beautiful mountain views. "Wake up," she would say. "Look at the snow on that mountain." It was July, it was hot. The back seat was crowded with the two old people and me, and I couldn't have cared less about scenery at that particular moment. "I've already seen a mountain,"I mumbled disagreeably.

The Pontiac began acting up the next day on the way into Salt Lake City. By nightfall it was necessary to seek out a garage for repair. Dad made arrangements with the owner to let him borrow tools and work on the engine. My father was a far better salesman than he was a mechanic. The owner turned the keys to the place over to Dad and said he'd see him in the morning.

Dad worked all night on the Pontiac grinding the valves, something he had apparently helped do not long before. At least this time he had all the necessary tools. With the mechanic's help for a short time the next morning, we were back on the road with a total cash repair outlay of $7.50.

Out in the Arizona desert we developed more problems. The car was running hot and we had emptied the canvas water bag that was hanging over the ornate radiator ornament in front of the radiator. Temperatures approached 120 degrees that day. Suddenly I smelled smoke. Our elderly passengers were both asleep in the back seat, where I was.

"Dad I smell something hot."

"Everything's hot, son," he replied, "It's probably just the engine overheating again."

The smell got noticeably stronger, but I held my comments. Soon however, smoke began to pour out from somewhere under the back seat.

"I think we're on fire!" I shouted, startling the old people awake.

"Something *is* burning," Old Bill said. "Where's my cigarette?"

Dad made as rapid a stop as the Pontiac's two-wheel, mechanical brakes permitted, which seemed to be about half a mile on the slight downhill grade. By the time we got out of the car the back seat was ablaze. Dad knew the emergency car water supply was dry and we had emptied all the drinking water earlier. The only thing he could find in the cooler chest was a quart of milk, which he promptly dumped on the seat. This made for a disgusting mess, but did put out the fire.

See what I mean about poor choices? But, if you are in the middle of the desert with no water and your car is on fire, you make do with the best thing you have. It is conceivable that in a few years we could be reaching that situation with automotive fuels.

At present it appears that ethanol (often called gasohol) may be the safest and best fuel extender. However, ethanol is not suitable as a fuel in itself for a number of reasons, not the least of which is that, it just won't start a car engine very well, if at all, when temperatures are below about forty degrees. Used in a ratio of ten-percent ethanol and unleaded gasoline, often called "super unleaded," it acts to increase octane ratings and reduce certain exhaust system pollutants, without vehicle starting problems.

The principal advantage to ethanol mixture fuels is that the grain alcohol (ethanol) is said to be a renewable resource.

Much of it is made from corn, although it can also efficiently be produced from sorghums, sugar cane, and other crops. There is a catch here as well. What powers the tractor doing the spring field work and planting the corn itself? Fuels made from oil. What is the fertilizer made from that produces the huge crop yields? Oil. What is the base of many of the chemicals that are in the herbicides and insecticides that control weeds and insects in the corn fields? Oil. What powers the combine that harvests the corn in the fall? Oil. What fuels the trucks that transport the grain for storage? Oil. What provides the huge amounts of heat for the stills that turn the corn into fuel alcohol? Often it too is a fossil fuel. What fuels the trucks that transport the fuel to distribution centers for mixing? Oil.

The question then is, is ethanol really a renewable resource after all? Many scientists at present are not even certain whether we can show a net energy gain from the production of grain alcohol. However, most Americans would certainly favor paying the money to our farmers rather than subsidizing some Middle East oil sheik. Unfortunately, if there's no net energy gain, we're still going to be paying the sheik the same amount, plus the subsidies to our farmers.

Once we find a way to use the grain alcohol itself to provide all the other power needed to produce the alcohol additive, we will have an enormous power gain. There may be help on the way to solve part of this problem. Recently the huge John Deere farm machinery company showed off a powerful rotary engine to power farm equipment. It is designed to run on diesel, gasoline, jet fuel or alcohol. Unfortunately, even if the latter fuel works in the engine satisfactorily, and the rotary goes into full production, it would be at least a decade or perhaps even two before really significant change would come about. This is because farm equipment remains in service for very long periods of time. Phasing in a totally new engine technology would take well into the twenty-first century. However, such developments would then be a major reason to consider corn produced ethanol as the top contender. Ethanol would then certainly be a renewable, low pollution resource.

So far that's not possible, or economically feasible, even with the highly subsidized ethanol projects working today. That subsidy amounts to about fourteen cents per gallon depending upon the state you live in. Remember, it still represents an ingredient that is usually only ten percent of the actual final fuel. Furthermore, cost illustrations do not include the actual crop, water, and electric subsidies now being paid directly to the farmer. These add substantially to the eventual ethanol cost.

Then we have to consider whether we should use another precious commodity—fresh water—to irrigate crops that are to be used for fuel. Extensive use of grain alcohol as a fuel will result in presently idled crop acres and marginal production crop ground being put back in use to raise more government subsidized grain.

However, if grain prices were to increase substantially because of using it to make a fuel, it is possible that all these government payments could be removed. Then we could start to make more economic sense out of ethanol. You can see there are a lot of "ifs" in this, and no easy answers to what our automobile fuel of the future may be.

Where do we go from there? Hydrogen presents an appealing choice, since it is made from water, even ocean water. As yet a practical way to transfer the fuel to the car's tank is a major problem, as is on-board storage, which is even more difficult and complex than propane and natural gas. If perfected, hydrogen would provide an almost limitless fuel source. That is likely to be many, many years into the future, unless some spectacular scientific breakthrough occurs.

Solar cells to produce electricity for vehicle power are another possibility, but as yet the technology just isn't available to make sufficiently efficient cells to collect enough power from the sun to do the job. These later alternative power sources for cars certainly deserve study and research. The problem is that we need a new energy source soon, if we really want to be independent of foreign oil.

The fuel cell which uses a chemical reaction to produce electricity is another laboratory-proven, but highly costly possibility. Another approach which may be the earliest contender could be a hybrid car. Perhaps it will use a very small, extremely efficient, gasoline engine, powered by alcohol mixtures to charge more efficient batteries that will in turn provide the actual driving power. At present, about all we have gotten done is to disagree on which of the known possible approaches is the best. We want to use less gasoline, preserve other vital resources such as fresh water, and create less pollution all at the same time.

Back in 1970, before gasoline shortages or its price was even considered when purchasing a car by most of us, I was still among those drivers very well pleased with my American Motors products. Perhaps they didn't have the styling panache or the brute horsepower of some other models, but they were at least as dependable as most, and the lighter weight of their unit body resulted in better gas mileage than most other cars.

That was just a money-saving quality back then, not a nation-threatening situation. Yet the car I was considering buying ran only on high-octane, premium-leaded gasoline.

Rambler sales were falling on tough times. Although Rambler had been building cars under one name or another since 1902, they did not seem to be able to capture enough market share to become a highly profitable company. In an effort to show the public that they were not just for old ladies to drive to church on Sunday, or Grandpa Snazzy to tour the cornfields, the company came out with a two-passenger vehicle called the AMC. This was a drag-racing model that held the fastest time in its class for a while. It was a pretty poor excuse for a car. Maybe it wasn't supposed to be a car, but rather an advertising symbol for speed and power.

The 1971 Rambler Ambassador was a car designed to

bridge the gap to the high-performance sedan market. Too few were built too late to turn around the ultimate fate of American Motors. The company had been building small (standard-sized by today's reduced measurements), gas-mileage-efficient vehicles as the major part of their business. Now, at almost the precise wrong moment, they switched to the high-performance large car, the model that died for all car manufacturers with the 1973 oil squeeze and subsequent government regulations.

I bought the Ambassador when the '71 models were first introduced in the fall of 1970. Few people could foresee the fuel shortage and its aftermath. The car had several attributes that appealed to my masculinity, yet had comfort for the five in our family. It still retained the individuality I prized in a vehicle, but within a more subdued styling. The front end looked something like a Jaguar.

The wheelbase on the "little" Rambler Ambassador was 122 inches, nearly the same as a Lincoln Town Car or Cadillac Fleetwood built today. I ordered a car with the "police interceptor package." This was mostly an upgrade to stiffer suspension, a larger alternator, stainless steel dual exhausts, and some internal engine parts built from tempered metals. It had more drive-train noise than the larger styles. Unit body models always transmitted a bit more road noise. Today with computer-engineered design, much of this has been taken out of current makes.

On my car, the big 401-cubic-inch V-8 engine was not designed to be silent. It was a fun-to-drive sedan, with a zero-to-sixty MPH time of just over seven seconds. This was almost unbelievable, particularly for a car with Rambler's staid reputation. That acceleration is quite respectable for most sports cars today or for any of the huge-engined models built back then. Cadillac put a 500-cubic-inch engine in a model that came out about that time. Of course, it was much heavier and larger than the Ambassador and therefore was much slower and more fuel thirsty. Nonetheless, the Caddy, and all other Ford, GM, and Chrysler products at the top end of the line were very fast. Of course this was during the days of the seventy-five mile per hour speed limit on interstate highways.

When the city of Kearney, Nebraska, our nearby neighbor, evaluated cars for their police fleet, they were greatly surprised to find a contender from American Motors. They ended up buying all of their "police interceptor models" from the Rambler dealer. In fact that was how I had learned that the special model Ambassador was available to the general public, although dressed up in respectable civilian apparel.

I happened to see the chief of police in the dealership one day. He had brought his police car in for routine service, just as I had.

"How are the Ambassadors working out for you?" I asked. "Well, we were having a lot of trouble with them to begin with, because we were driving them flat-out a lot of the time," he replied.

"What was breaking down?" I was very curious now since I also owned one. Maybe some extra preventive maintenance would help with any problems.

"Oh, no," he laughed, "Nothing mechanical. They've been great for us in that respect. It's just that every kid in the country who thinks he has a fast car, looks at the police driving Ramblers and tries to outrun us!"

He chuckled again. "Word just didn't seem to be getting around that we were catching all of them. I suspect they were reluctant to tell their friends they got caught by a Rambler. Furthermore, those darned high-speed chases are always dangerous, and we were getting more than our share."

"So have you got a solution?" I wondered.

"Yeah. One of our officers got the idea. You know we put on programs once or twice a year for the schools. Jack let it be known to the high school students and the college kids that we were going to do some special time trials on our new patrol vehicles." He smiled. "Then he sent written invitations to all the car clubs. At the time, the best place we had where we could limit our liability was blocking off a section of interstate at about 2 A.M. Didn't have as big a crowd as we would have liked, but the effect was the same, because we got to the right people.''

"So what did you do?'' I asked expectantly.

"We set up several radar units, calibrated everything and ran two or three of our Ambassadors through the traps. You should have seen the looks on those kids' faces when we clocked a consistent 135 to 140 miles an hour, and those zero-to-sixty times in the seven-second range. Within a day or so we just didn't have anybody trying us, which was fine with me. We were going through tires like crazy!''

There were a couple of other surprising things about that car. Vehicles of its size that could approximate its speed averaged about eight to ten miles per gallon of gas. On the road, at speeds of 75 MPH, the legal interstate speed, I was getting a consistent sixteen to eighteen, and it didn't tail off much around town because the Ambassador was 600 pounds lighter than most of its competitors.

The second thing wasn't as pleasing. The car used a full quart of oil about every 500 miles. Despite the fact I had it worked on while still under warranty, it continued to use oil. Then, with about 50,000 on the odometer, it stopped using any oil at all between changes and never used any thereafter!

I asked my dealer what was going on.

"You finally got it broke in, huh?'' Pete said. "Seems the police fleet had the same problem as you did, only it didn't last as long. The hours of idling plus all those high-speed chases made the alloy block and tempered engine rings seat in fairly quickly. None of them burned any oil once they got broke in.''

Pete no longer sold new cars when the downturn in sales of American Motors products became more pronounced.

"Why don't you pick up a dealership with some other good name?'' I questioned.

"After having a Nash dealership in the family for almost

fifty years, it just doesn't feel right to start selling something else. Besides, I'm getting too old to fight all the dealership problems, and come up with that kind of cash outlay,'' Pete told me. That ended my long-term association with Nash-Rambler-American Motors products.

I remember asking Pete on an earlier occasion just what was covered by the new ''12 month or 12,000'' mile warranty on new cars that most of the industry had adopted.

''What do you care?'' he asked bluntly. ''You've never had a car we didn't fix under our personal warranty if the manufacturer didn't stand behind it.''

He was right. That's why his loss as my dealer of choice was deeply regretted. But Pete just couldn't continue doing business that way. I'm sure a competent, friendly dealer has a great deal to do with any car purchase. I know it did with mine.

I continued driving the Ambassador for several years, until it had well over 135,000 miles on it. When I sold it outright for $1,000, it was still in excellent condition. The major problem was that the engine required the very highest octane, leaded gasoline to satisfy its ten-to-one compression ratio. With regulations coming that would eliminate leaded fuel for cars altogether, and the fact that the new gasolines wouldn't have high enough octane, I reluctantly parted with the car. Considering that I drove it for more than eight years, and the fully equipped car sold new with a sticker price of $4,950, it may have been the only bargain vehicle I ever owned.

Dogs are usually better travelers than children. They're so entranced by all the sights and sounds going by the windows that they never ask the question, ''How soon are we going to get there?'' With kids, this questions comes the instant you have shifted into forward gear from reverse when backing out of the driveway. This is absolutely, always, positively followed by ''What's to eat (drink, do)?'', and that great car stopper,''

"I've got to go to the bathroom."

Now I'm not making any sort of comparison of traveling companions here, although I do admit that I can relate to the feelings of W. C. Fields when he said, "Anyone who hates dogs and little kids can't be all bad." I don't agree with him about dogs. Some dogs, that is. Even a few children enjoy traveling, or at least like the concept of going somewhere. They just tire of it rapidly. The ones who fight constantly to avoid boredom and harass the driver receive my ire. (I exclude my own grandchildren, of course, who never do anything outrageous in a car, like standing on the seats with muddy feet, pushing, pulling, twisting, turning, sliding, screwing, or bending every available knob, button, handle or lever.)

Our dog, Dusty, was an excellent traveler. She was supposed to be a German short-hair, however her small size and black coloring, with typical short-hair ticking on her chest, brought this into question. The vet said it was not totally unusual to get throwbacks in genetics in a dog that was a relatively new breed. I suspected that our new breed dog was half German short-hair and half some kind of terrier. She was the runt of the litter, but made up for it with a very alert mind.

Out of the same litter of pups a friend bought a large, very definite short-hair male. The problem with Ace was that over the years he never even learned his own name. Fortunately, he at least had the looks of a champion.

Dusty, on the other hand, was the only dog I have ever owned that could be trained to do almost any trick or hunting tactic by just seeing it once. Usually, dog training is a matter of "reps." Any good football coach will tell you these are repetitions, an absolute essential in training players to do something right. My wife Ardelle, in her surprisingly sheltered life on the farm, never had a pet of any kind, and certainly no house dogs. One day she was baking cookies and yelled at me with a great deal of urgency in her voice.

"Dusty just talked to me!"

"Great. We'll never have to work again the rest of our lives."

She ignored my comment. "All right, Dusty, do it again," she said, extending a freshly baked cookie in the dog's direction. Dusty went through her entire repertoire of cute things to do to get a treat, including whining and barking.

"So," I said, "What did you think she said?"

"I didn't think it, I know it," Ardelle insisted. "That dog

said 'Dusty wants a cookie' just as plain as could be!''

Although to the best of my knowledge, the wonder dog never spoke again, Ardelle has.

From a very young age, Dusty could be sleeping two rooms away, hear the words ''car'' or ''truck'' in normal conversational tones and dash back and forth between whoever said the magic word and the nearest door in a matter of seconds. It is the rare dog that does not like to ride in a vehicle. They especially like to stand with their heads sticking out of the window, ears and hair flopping wildly in the wind, tongues lolling out their mouths, and nose getting splattered with bugs, looking for all the world like motorcyclists.

Here in our little town of Holdrege we have always had a preponderance of people whose last name is Johnson. This is not a particularly unusual situation since Johnson is the second most common last name in the entire United States. However, I thought about this in connection with the observations about car-riding dogs, because it brought to mind ''Three-Dog Johnson.'' Many Johnsons had to have nicknames to separate them from other identically named Johnsons. Three-Dog Johnson was so named because of the variety of farm dogs, usually at least six or more, that were always in the cab and box of his pickup. Whether the people who nicknamed him couldn't count because the intermarriage among Johnsons was so high, or whether Three-Dog had moved up a few notches in dog population, I don't really know. I do know that having made these remarks, it is a good thing my Swedish grandmother was named Johnson.

The thing about our dog Dusty was that she not only knew her own name so well that we had to be careful in spelling it out if our conversation had anything to do with a ride in a vehicle, she also seemed to sense what we were talking about.

''Are we going to take the d-o-g in the c-a-r?'' worked for a while. No doubt we were giving some sort of visual or sound clue she would pick up on. Once in the car I could say, ''Look at all the cows (or ducks or whatever)!'' and she would obediently jump up and search the fields until she found what we were looking at.

Although Dusty never talked to me, she could make her presence known in other ways. When in the car, after the initial excitement had worn off, she would settle down in the front seat, always resting her head on my right leg with her tail touching Ardelle. In this relaxed position she would pass incredible amounts of doggie gas, an endearing trick Ardelle would not tolerate.

"Phew, Dusty. You stink!"

The dog would rouse herself, ears drooping and sad eyes looking at Ardelle, knowing that she was being relegated to the floor of the car. It was impossible for her to see outside from this position. It also did not provide the high level of sleeping comfort. Repeated banishments to the floor soon improved her car manners amazingly.

When we bought a twenty-seven-foot camping trailer, it became obvious that our second car should really be a truck. We needed the extra towing and carrying capacity. The International Travelall was supposed to be a vehicle with the nearly perfect shape for hauling numerous four-by-eight-foot sheets of plywood flat on the floor, and yet having a ride like a car. I say supposed to be, because my 1972 Travelall just reversed that. It rode like a lumber wagon and pulled a big trailer as poorly as a car.

This unit was built by International Harvester, the farm equipment company. It had a luggage rack on top and a 392-cubic-inch V-8 engine. The specifications seemed to be there to do the job we wanted, but somehow it just didn't work right. The suspension was far too lightweight to handle heavy loads, and the engine, transmission and rear-end ratio seemed to be fighting each other. In fact, it had everything I wasn't looking for in a towing vehicle. The engine didn't have nearly the power its size would indicate, and yet the gas mileage was awful. We're talking four and five miles to the gallon, not even the usual eight or better you can expect from most big block engines pulling RV rigs.

I'll summarize my relationship with this vehicle by telling you something that happened to me years before. It was while I was employed at KGFW radio and had worked my way up to chief announcer. In those days, radio newscasts were much longer, and everything was live, even the commercials. If news broadcasts were done correctly, it was necessary to put quite a bit of preparation into each newscast, particularly in reading over the stories to be sure of pronunciations and context.

The sports man and I worked as a two-man team. I handled all the world, state, and local news, in addition to weather, he did the commercials during my segments and then took over with the sports while I read the spots. At our station, the man in the announcer's booth also had control of all microphones and other equipment. The guy in the studio with the overhead mike did not have to worry about switching or volume levels. In fact he couldn't even turn off the studio mike. I usually worked in the booth.

There is frequently an unheard aside going on during radio broadcasts. One announcer tries to break up the other on air with gestures, grimaces, or props of some kind. This is a challenge that professionals can handle and enjoy knowing that listeners usually have no idea what is going on.

A few months earlier, while Morey, our sports man, was in the middle of his segment, I had ridden a bicycle into the plush carpeted third-floor studio, and I continued to sit on the bicycle in front of the microphone while an enormous quantity of teletype news off the wire piled up in the bike basket. I proceeded to edit it for broadcast. There was nothing uproariously funny about this except in the context of the totally unexpected. Out of the corner of his eye Morey had watched this silent, improbable situation unfold.

Gradually he broke up, with slight chuckles becoming huge guffaws, until he had to shut off his mike. After that, I didn't have to do much more than look at him and he would have a hard time controlling his reaction. Through all our time together, he had never succeeded in breaking me up on air. He hated that.

On a particular morning I had been out of the station doing a remote broadcast and didn't return until very near air time for my noon newscast. It was so late, in fact, that all I had time to do was rush into the teletype room, rip off a huge long sheet of unread news and weather, and head for the mike. I realized that sitting in the announcer's booth and handling this lengthy page would make an incredible amount of noise on the air, so I told the sportscaster to take the booth and I would work from a stand-up mike out in the studio.

Things seemed to be going along quite well. Morey was riding gain on my mike while I was keeping one eye on the second hand and trying to get through the unprepared news with few errors. Then I became aware of movement from the booth. Morey opened the door, leaving my mike on, and came out into the studio. He smiled, took out his cigarette lighter, and set the entire bottom of my long sheet of news ablaze. He sat down calmly to watch, knowing that I hated dead air-time, yet I could not shut off my microphone. He had me.

This incident gave a whole new meaning to hot news. It also provided an authentic sense of impending disaster. Fortunately, I was able to scan ahead on the sheet, drop the flaming mess on the carpeted floor, and stomp out the fire while I ad libbed the rest of the story. Morey still didn't break me up. I should have been so lucky with my Travelall.

The feeling was exactly the same. Our new trailer was pulling all right, yet I sensed impending disaster. The fan clutch squawked and howled before locking up completely. The result was overheating the engine, with no way to drive the vehicle into the nearest town. There we were, Ardelle, our three daughters, the dog and me, stranded on the interstate and hooked on to a trailer. A friendly trucker summoned help and a wrecking truck towed us in to the nearest garage for repairs.

Although this was the only time we were unable to limp in under our own power, we had four more of these breakdowns during the same trip. The left rear wheel bearing went out near the next small town. Come on, how many rear wheel bearings have you ever had go out on a vehicle? That's pretty rare. Luckily they had the parts to fix it. Then the right one went out just a few more miles down the road. When the engine began to miss badly in the next twenty miles, it turned out to be a faulty coil. Next the muffler blew off, making us sound like a tractor, perhaps harking back to the origins of this vehicle. All the repairs and tow-ins took hours. In fact, we covered just 150 miles in some eighteen hours before giving up. We had more than had it with the Travelall.

I had been shopping halfheartedly for a better tow vehicle, but now I got mad, went into the small town dealer where we had been stopped for the night, and after minimum negotiations, bought a new Chevy Suburban. This is not a wise way to trade vehicles. Impulsiveness is not the friend of the car driver and certainly not of the new car buyer.

I'll always remember a couple of impetuous actions that happened with friends of mine, so it wasn't like I didn't know better than to rush into something half-cocked. One man, I jokingly referred to as Dr. Jeckyl and Mr. Hart had a complete change of personality the moment he got behind the wheel of his car. Riding with someone else, driving annoyances didn't seem to bother him, and he was a normal, friendly guy in any other situation.

On this particular day, on a downtown four-lane street, a young driver roared by us and cut in front of Dr. Jeckyl so sharply that the good doctor had to land on his brakes hard, to keep from hitting the inconsiderate motorist. The driver was the first car in line at an upcoming stop light, when I saw Mr. Hart take over the wheel. He coasted up behind the show-off driver without slowing down. I braced myself for the impact, and looked in horror at the glint of glee in Al Hart's eyes. The crash came at only about five miles an hour, but sent the rival driver careening across a fortunately empty intersection. I didn't ride with Al much after that.

The second instance was with a high school principal. Bud loved to hunt pheasants and invited me up to go out with him. Normally, if you go hunting with someone you don't really know well, you're pretty safe, as long as you stay away from large groups, or people who say, "How about a couple shots of blackberry brandy, just to warm up a bit before we go get 'em."

This expedition didn't fit either of those patterns. Bud had a new Plymouth, and it was just the two of us going out in the late afternoon. Since I liked to walk out in the fields to flush the birds, I was surprised when Bud began to "road hunt." This practice is against the law. It means driving very slowly down a gravel road and eyeballing the ditches, which I must admit to having done a few times when pheasants were plentiful, but never this way. Suddenly, Bud jerked open his door with one hand like a man possessed, grabbed his shotgun, leaped to the ground, and began shooting almost immediately at three rooster pheasants.

I really didn't have time to look. I lunged over to the driver's side to grab the steering wheel and brake, as the driverless car stopped just inches from the ditch. Bud returned in a minute, proudly carrying a rooster pheasant.

"How in hell did you manage to shoot that quickly?" I asked in amazement. I knew how he had bailed out of the car without concern for the result, and shot the pheasant while standing in the middle of the road, but he accomplished these things in some sort of never-before-seen speed record.

"Always keep her fully loaded," he said. This guy was very calm under most school or business situations and didn't appear at all excitable.

"I just remembered," I said, "I've got to get back to town right away before the bank closes." It was the best excuse I could come up with.

"I'll pick you up Friday for that meeting over in Hastings,"

Bud reminded me as I got into my own car.

"Fine," I replied, "7 A.M."

On Friday Bud was right on schedule, but was driving an old car I had never seen before.

"Where'd you get this clunker? Want to take mine?" I asked.

"Yeah, might be a good idea. The new one's in the shop," he replied.

"What's wrong with it?" I quizzed.

"Having the front seat worked on, and the passenger door."

"All warranty stuff then," I pressed. He didn't seem too anxious to tell me what was wrong with the new car.

"No. Ah, damn! I just as well tell you. You're going to find out anyway," he said shamefacedly. "I went out hunting by myself, saw some pheasants on that same road we were on the other day, jumped out the door, got tangled up with the blasted gun, and blew off the right front half of the seat. The car ran into the ditch and took a mailbox right through the passenger door."

In retrospect, perhaps buying a new vehicle on the spur of the moment when I became infuriated with the Travelall's mechanical problems wasn't quite as stupid as some of the other things we drivers do.

# 11

# *Invasion of the Japanese Body Snatchers*

JUST IN CASE this chapter title makes you think of a cult movie, you're close. The plot of the movie dealt with aliens from outer space invading the bodies of earthlings and eventually taking over the minds of everyone in the world. In the real world, we've all read the headlines: "U.S. Trade Imbalance With the Japanese Is Growing" or "Japanese Students Surpass U.S. in Test Scores." And the one that galls some of us most of all: "Japanese Cars Rank Superior to U.S. Makes."

Many Americans who were born during the baby boom, or any time following World War II, are not aware of the prevalent attitude their older countrymen once had toward all things Japanese. Even before the war and during the postwar period of the late 1940s, Japanese workmanship and poor quality were listed in the thesaurus as synonyms.

There has always been a demand for imported goods. Those deemed of quality were made in Europe. We knew the British Empire made the best crystal, china, or sterling. Serious photographers thought that cameras made in Germany, such as the Rolleiflex or Speed Graphic, and Ziess lenses were the only equipment worthy of their consideration. The best watch movements were Swiss; France was famous for its fashion and its wine. The Italians, excelled in shoes and art.

What about automobiles? The English had the Rolls Royce and the Jaguar. The Germans crafted cars from the lowly Volkswagen to the haughty Mercedes Benz. The Italians built the Alfa Romeo and the Ferrari. Sweden chipped in with the Volvo. We saw few of these cars on our highways. They were generally owned by the scandalously rich, or in the case of the Volkswagen, the counterculture.

Deep down, we Americans knew that the real value for the dollar was in American-made automobiles. We had the prestige of the mighty Cadillac, the power and status of the Packard, and the engineering of the Chrysler. Most of us drove Fords, Plymouths, and Chevys—the ''Big Three'' as they were known—but we had a wide choice of other excellent cars including Hudsons, Nashes, Studebakers, and all the other products of the major companies.

Japanese *cars*? Are you kidding? All they made were dime-store trinkets. Something you bought only when you couldn't afford better quality. Automobiles? Do they even manufacture them?

Even after the Japanese attack on Pearl Harbor the general public never really considered the Japanese a major threat as we did the Germans. After all, we had better fighter planes than their Zeros. Their navy was little more than a ''scrap metal'' fleet. It was a very good thing that our propaganda helped us maintain that cocky attitude during the early years of World War II, for it was we, not the Japanese, who had the inferior equipment. It is equally true that our overwhelming ability to produce in quantity ultimately gave us superiority in armaments.

After Japan's defeat, we occupied that country somewhat magnanimously. Gen. Douglas MacArthur was largely responsible for establishing a Japanese constitution and government. He was able to do so because he (and we) believed that the Japanese were backward and easily led. We even "let" them keep their emperor as a figurehead. Rebuilding Japan so that it could get into the mainstream of the world economy was a priority in the late 1940s. Japanese self-sufficiency was our major concern

A 1950 *National Geographic* article by Frederick G. Vosburg was entitled "Japan Tries Freedom's Road." The question was, how could a nation only one-twentieth the size of the forty-eight states and possessing only "100 trails" for transportation, hope to compete?

Vosburg wrote, "Although Japan does make automobiles, the country has few by American standards. Muscle, not motors, propels many loads. Little trailers [are] hitched to some of Japan's 6,000,000 bicycles."

The Japanese diet then was largely rice, fish, and vegetables—a matter of some concern to Americans. Such a diet was obviously deficient in calcium and animal protein. This was given as the reason the Japanese were so small in stature compared to people like us. In fact, the American Occupation Public Health office reported that the average Japanese man was 5′3″ tall, while the average woman was only 4′11″. Perhaps we could do something to change their poor eating habits. Teach 'em to eat fried pork chops, fried potatoes, and lemon pie for dessert!

American influence was also evident in education. For the first time co-education was introduced. The Japanese thirst for knowledge was evident. It was just that most Americans never noticed. After all, how interested could you be in a society whose average monthly income was only about 10,000 yen, or twenty-eight American dollars. The lowest American private in the army of occupation made about triple that.

In the fifties we were very busy exporting western-style machinery, clothes and, believe it or not, radios, to Japan. We were teaching the Japanese what efficiency was all about. We had trimmed the excess employees of the Japanese railroads by 100,000, for example. "Wasteful," we observed, while our own railroad unions continued to fight for overstaffed trains, using the same "featherbedding" tactics we corrected in Japan.

One theory was that overpopulated Japan could never be competitive. Others thought that the labor force should be put to work repairing the nation's antiquated, bumpy road system. The Japanese agreed, but also developed an advanced system of trains and mass transit which now may be the best in the world.

The Japanese realized they had to export to live. The leading Japanese camera maker of the time began searching for new ideas to make its products acceptable worldwide. Looking back, it is amazing how fast the Japanese came to dominate the camera market. German lenses were just as good as they ever were, and the American Kodak was still everyman's simple camera. The Japanese simply built a more advanced product, cheaper.

In the 1950 *National Geographic* article, a leading Japanese industrialist was asked if Japan's future depended on America.

"Everything in Japan is fifteen years behind America," he said. "We respect America as an elder brother and follow in his ways."

The author wondered just how long America would continue its tutelage. He questioned whether it would be long enough for the teachings to stick. Then he mentioned something General MacArthur had said, "I believe the only thing in this world that can't be stopped is a sound idea. . . ."

Could anyone have foreseen that many American consumers would change from considering all Japanese goods inferior to purchasing everything from electronics to cars from Japan, because of the *quality*? Would any American have believed that his countrymen would completely change their thinking from believing that we should buy American—even if foreign products were better—because it was the patriotic thing to do?

There are still many places in rural United States where driving a foreign-made car is frowned upon. This attitude may seem old-fashioned, but as they so often have done in the past, the rural, conservative population of our nation may sense what's best for the nation. Fortunately, our cars have gained so much in quality in the past ten years that the major problem we need to overcome now is the same one the Japanese fought thirty years ago: the belief that the United States simply can't build a decent car!

Japan has forced us to be more competitive and innovative. We can thank our former "little brothers" for that awakening.

In the mid-1980s I had an opportunity to visit with a man in high level technical management with one of our leading car makers. Actually, Rob and his wife were staying in an RV parked beside us at a campground. Since they were on a short two-week vacation from the Motor City, I hated to bring up the subject of the car business, but because I might never have a similar chance again, I asked Rob if he minded talking shop. He assured me he didn't.

"Do you think American cars will ever be able to catch up with the Europeans in handling and quality?" I asked him.

"I spent three years in various European countries and my staff did a lot of taking apart and studying their methods of construction and engineering," he replied. "We're narrowing in on them now, and in another five years the designs we're working on for production will be very competitive with them at all levels."

He paused to consider that statement. "I don't mean that we'll be just competitive, I really believe we'll produce cars that are better engineered, for less money."

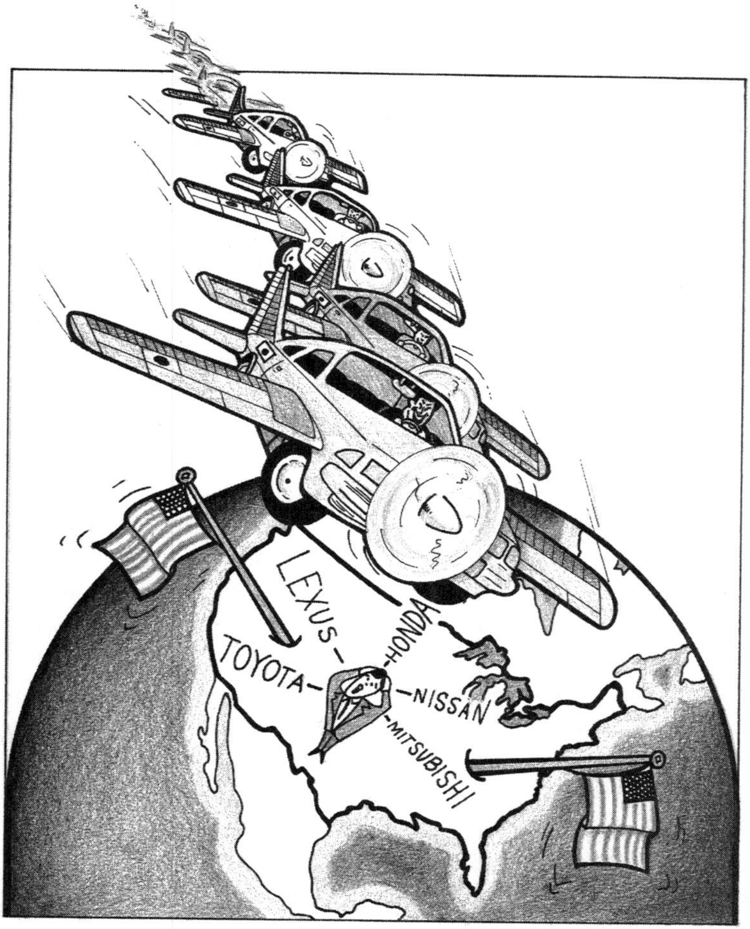


That caught me offguard. "Are you saying that you think American cars will be the world leaders?"

"No, that wasn't your question was it? You asked if I thought American cars would ever catch up with the Europeans." This was no gung-ho, mind-programed youngster I was talking to. In fact he was planning to retire soon. He looked at me thoughtfully, "Who really scares the hell out of me are the Japanese!"

"I know they're already the best in the small car market, but you're saying more than that?" I quizzed.

"I just got back from a year and a half in Japan, studying their production methods and their latest innovations. They're going to be real competitors, even in the luxury market, and not far down the line." Rob said.

"What are they doing differently?"

"They've got the most modern plants, extremely quick design change turn around, robotics, and good ergonomic sense." He smiled wryly. "I just wish I was going to stick around long enough in the business to see how it all shakes out. Right now they've still got us, and everybody else too. But we're going to make a run at them. It should be fun!" Rob laughed.

This conversation came after I had already owned a couple of Japanese cars and had returned to the American market. Frankly, I was surprised Rob was so candid and so confident. I had become extremely disenchanted with the 1970s quality of American-made vehicles, but he seemed to think we were turning the corner.

A few years earlier I had written letters to each of the major car makers with my complaints, warning them that this faithful purchaser of American cars was just about mad enough to buy an overseas product. At the time of my disgust, I had just purchased a 1978 Chevy Suburban. I was so disappointed in this new factory-ordered unit that I vowed I would not buy another American-made vehicle until they listened to some common sense about quality control.

They didn't.

My Suburban had misaligned body panels and a rear tailgate window that could be rolled down only sometimes. The paint had "orange peel" in it where it had been sprayed over greasy surfaces. The windshield cracked immediately and was replaced three times before it was discovered that a piece of weld had been dropped into the windshield channel at the factory, causing the breaks.

The truck would die after a long drive and refuse to start for periods of about twenty minutes, then fire up as if nothing had happened. The radio worked poorly, the cruise control went out, and the air conditioner didn't cool.

There were many other problems, the most important of which was the use of a quart of oil about every 200 miles. When I complained about this, my dealer told me, "All Chevys with a 454 engine use oil like that."

I didn't buy his excuse. "Mine's not going to," I told him.

His shop worked on the problem several times without results. I kept on putting in oil. I began to suspect that the repair work may have consisted of the old "fresh air and sunshine treatment." Let the car sit in the lot for a couple days and hope that the problem will go away. Finally, someone decided I was not going to accept the "they all do it" reasoning. Arrangements were made for a factory rep to check out the problem.

"I think I know what's wrong," he confided, "Let's take it out on the road and check it."

We left the garage and headed out on the highway. "Get in back and watch out the rear window, will you?" He speeded up to about sixty and took his foot off the gas pedal. A huge cloud of blue smoke made it look like we were fogging for mosquitos.

"Lots of blue smoke when you decelerated," I told him.

"OK. That's what I thought." he smiled, "You've got bad valve seals."

"But this is a new truck," I protested.

"That's true, but we've been having a lot of trouble with seals put in wrong, sometimes even missing altogether. Would you believe that I checked an engine over in Kearney yesterday where none of the valve seals had been put in at all! You think you've got oil problems. That guy couldn't pour quart cans of oil in fast enough to keep up if the engine was running!"

"How big a job is it to fix?" I asked.

"Maybe a couple hours or so. We've got a special tool so it doesn't require much disassembly," he explained. "Probably at least half of the 454's engines have the same problem. Maybe this was built on a Monday or Friday. Bad days for assembly line workers. A lot of them are either coming in with a terrible hangover or getting ready for another weekend."

"So that's why they told me *all* these engines use oil," I thought to myself. This whole episode was not confidence inspiring. Subconsciously I had already made the decision to buy a foreign make.

Some of the problems with the Chevy were simply design flaws which had not been corrected despite more than five years of building this same model. I'm not picking on Chevrolet. Poor quality in American cars at the time was endemic. This just happened to be the one I had bought. The International Harvester Travelall I had sold when I bought the Suburban was listed by *Popular Mechanics* owner surveys among the worst vehicles in several categories. I would agree with that. It seemed I had a knack for buying the worst of the worst. Many other owners obviously had "Corn Binder" troubles too. The International was nicknamed that because of its notoriously noisy performance on the road, and the fact that it was manufactured by a company known primarily for its farm equipment and large diesel trucks. The Travelall disappeared as a production model even before I parted with mine. That meant little value in my vehicle as a resale. It was another lesson in the financial disasters stalking car owners.

I think back to my own employment history of craftsmanship. My father was adamant about me having part-time jobs while in school. He arranged for one job in the furniture department of Sears Roebuck. At the time I was about 125 pounds and slightly less than six feet tall. I was no ninety-eight pound weakling, like those depicted in the Charles Atlas muscle building ads of the time.

The Sears job involved moving 200- to 300-pound rolls of carpet from the unloading docks to the second floor without a great deal of mechanical assistance. It wasn't too tough to wheel the dollies carrying the carpet rolls onto the elevator, which was a "manual" freight elevator.

A thick rope revolved around a pulley far overhead and, through some unseen gearing mechanism, pulling the rope either raised or lowered the entire elevator. It was pretty simple if there were just one or two people on the elevator. When you got a couple big rolls of carpet on board, moving from the alley level to the second floor was a tough job. I had to jump up and pull for all I was worth to gain a few feet. However, I did manage to unload dozens of rolls of carpet at the second-floor level during my tenure.

I never seemed to get to take the carpet *down* the elevator. This worked the same as going up, except you used the other side of the rope and had the easy job of lowering it with the weight working for you. For some reason, the full-time employees always seemed to be the ones taking carpet down, and I was always the one taking it up. In fairness, I will say that this job made me a rope-climbing star in school gym class.

I always knew it would come, however—my turn to take the elevator down with several huge rolls of carpet. A wooden handle locked the elevator at the floor level while loading. I pushed the dollies onto the elevator, anticipating the easy ride down.

I released the handle and the load suddenly plummeted. I grabbed the spinning rope and only succeeded in burning my hands. There was a sudden stop, a lot of bouncing up and down on the emergency springs, and here we were—ropes tangled, gears stripped, and an unserviceable elevator.

Surprisingly, my Sears job didn't end there. I was reassigned to the unassembled furniture department. I don't like to think the fact that Dad was a good friend of the manager had anything to do with this.

My job was assembling the display pieces. Apparently Dad had told his friend that I had taken woodworking in school. I doubt that he mentioned that I had nearly flunked it. I know you will find that hard to believe. Nobody flunks junior high school woodworking.

My sole project had been a lap writing table for my grandmother, built from a piece of three-eighths-inch plywood. We were to cut a fairly large piece of plywood into a rectangle. Next, using a coping saw, we cut a semi-circle in it, about the size of the person you're building it for. We then had to file it smooth, sand it, finish it, and give it away. I worked on it all semester.

I never seemed to be able to get the hole quite even, as my instructor was prone to point out to me daily. So I would measure, eyeball it, and go at it with the wood rasp again. Then the bell would ring, I would put it away, and the instructor again the next day would point out the fact that the semi-circle was not even. I used several different pieces of plywood.

Finally it was done to my teacher's satisfaction—or exasperation. It was a good thing, too. There was only about a three-inch space remaining in front of the would-be-writer.

"My grandma is awfully fat," I told the woodwork czar, in an attempt to explain the huge hole in the writing desk. "Besides, look at the great finish I put on it and all that space to write she'll have on both sides of her."

"The circle's still not even," he said, rolling his eyes. He gave me a D- because he was afraid my parents might make me repeat the class if I got an F.

However, my boss at Sears didn't know that. He gave me some hand tools, a counter to store stuff, and told me to assemble a cupboard for display. This was a real step up. I had my own little area to work in and nobody to bother me. Then I got a look at the box this thing came in. There were pieces and pieces and pieces. I worked on that monster for two or three weeks, having no trouble laying out the dozens of parts, and fitting the drawers together. Actually, I was quite good at that.

The whole thing was supposed to be put together with screws of assorted sizes and driving them into that hard wood was a terrific task. I had learned how to do this from watching my father. Dad treated screws like fat nails and drove them in with a hammer. This didn't work badly on soft wood, except for the fact they often came right back out.

This was the method I tried on the unfinished kitchen cupboard. I could drive them in part of the way, but then it was like beating on sheet steel. I got a bigger hammer. I could see I was going to have to figure out how to improve on Dad's screw-driving method. Perhaps that was what a screw driver was for!

Thus, two advanced technologies were combined. Driving the screws in as far as they would go with my hammer, I then went at them with the screw driver until my hands were raw. Downstairs in the clothing department I bought a pair of work gloves and returned to my project.

Finally the job was completed. With help from the part-time worker who had taken over my carpet hauling job, I moved the big cupboard out onto the sales floor. In less than five minutes the department head was back in my room.

"Just what do you expect me to do with that thing?" he demanded. "Do you think anybody's going to buy unassembled furniture if its going to look like that when it's done?" He pointed to screw heads protruding at various odd angles. "Don't you know how to use a drill?"

As a matter of fact, I didn't. He showed me how to drill the holes straight with a slightly smaller hole than the screw threads. The somewhat longer screws went in quite easily, and held better, too. What would they think of next?

I've often wondered if some of the people who worked on the American auto assembly lines during the 1970s were products of the same level of training I had in my attempt to put that unfinished cupboard together.

Did you know that Sears once sold brand-new automobiles in their larger stores and through their catalog? They were called (you're probably ahead of me on this) the "All State."

Think this was right after they stopped selling buggy whips? Guess again.

In the early fifties the Henry J. Kaiser Automobile Company built cars for Sears. Actually, it was probably a desperation move by Kaiser. He had designed an especially ugly little car he called the Henry J. The public ignored it in droves. He then hit upon the idea of mass marketing the car through Sears tire and battery shops, but that didn't work either.

Kaiser had built a huge aluminum and ship building empire earlier, but the American automobile industry baffled him. He was quoted in newspapers as saying, "This is the only industry in the world where you can drop in more than $300 million dollars and watch it disappear without a ripple!"

The all-time worst results in the *Popular Mechanics* owner's survey for poorest quality went to the 1958 Lincoln, until the Yugo was imported in the 1980s. The Yugo just about swept the field, including worst dealer service. Not all foreign cars are well made by any means.

The 1970 Plymouth Barracuda took worst ever in fuel economy with an overall average of 8.7 miles per gallon, but it was in a tight finish with the 1972 Cadillac Eldorado.

The best ever overall rating went to the 1956 Mercedes Benz 300 SL. You have to go back to the 1955 to find the number-two finisher. It was Packard, the American luxury car that's no longer built. Recently, a Japanese luxury car, the Lexus, topped the survey in three major categories. In fact the owners placed Japanese cars at the top of many categories over the past fifteen years. But even Lexus couldn't beat the ninety-seven percent of Packard owners surveyed who indicated that car was best in overall quality.

Unfortunately, Packard made a marketing mistake when it tried to penetrate the middle-price range by cheapening a vehicle that had always been considered very upscale. The Packard held on in various strange forms until Studebaker bought the company and turned out a garish vehicle with the Packard nameplate on it. The car bore no resemblance to the high-quality vehicles of previous years. Mercifully, the old Packard nameplate died.

Perhaps the worst thing about American vehicles built during the decade of the 1970s was that nobody seemed to care. This created buyer frustration of the highest order. The American car market was wide open to anyone who would produce a car more in tune with the times and with reasonable quality.

Even military veterans, like me, were disgruntled. Wrapping the flag around an auto purchase only worked for so long. We became like the man in the bitterly satirical movie of 1976, *Network*. We simply stuck our heads out of a window and yelled, "I'm mad as hell, and I'm not going to take it anymore!"

Old advertising tricks no longer satisfied most car buyers. The 1970s was certainly the low point for American-built cars. Even much-improved U.S. cars from the mid 1980s into the 1990s are still trying to live down a reputation for lack of quality that has been overcome.

As my personal protest, I bought a 1980 Datsun 510 as a second car. It was inexpensive, but had a quirky manual transmission with a strange gearshift pattern. Fuel economy was excellent, but the durability and overall quality weren't nearly as good as I had expected from a Japanese-built automobile. This was especially true with the second owner, as I followed the car's history after I sold it.

The 1982 Nissan (a name change by Datsun that year) was much improved. The "hatchback" model had plenty of hauling capacity when the back seat was folded down, excellent economy with its five-speed transmission, and good durability. However, it was somewhat short on creature comforts for a six-footer. It also did not corner very well, had a choppy highway ride, and repair costs were high.

Other Japanese cars were several steps ahead. They continued to come up with more and better models, even, more recently, luxury cars. However, I decided that five years of protest against American manufacturers was enough. Quality level was improving in this country, and I found a car I liked in the 1984 Pontiac STE.

This car was based on the General Motors body shared by all the separate divisions, but was decked out in European styling, braking, and handling. The engine was a slightly underpowered 2.8 liter V-6 coupled to a three-speed automatic transmission. Nonetheless, the STE was a good package, lacking only fuel injection to provide an easier starting engine.

This purchase relates in a way to an experience I had in junior high school. As you know, Dad thought I should work part-time after school and during the summer. Mother insisted I continue taking lessons in the dancing class where I had been enrolled since I was about five years old. Although he never said so, I had the feeling that Dad thought tap dancing would turn me into a sissy. They compromised. I got to work *and* take dancing lessons.

My mother had taken over as the piano player for the neophyte dancers. It was a job she liked, and at which she was extremely good. There are thousands of good piano players, but not many who can read through a song once, or just hear somebody hum it, and be able to play it in any key from then on.

Apparently I had a pretty good sense of rhythm from an early age, because any tempo variation, however necessary to the would-be dancer's performance, drove me crazy. Despite my protests that I hated tap dancing, Mother wouldn't let me quit. She said I needed it because I was shy, quiet, clumsy, and couldn't remember anything. Tap dancing would help bring me out of this slack-jawed stupidity, she assured me. Mother was a real ego builder. I thought she had a "Mother of Fred Astaire" complex.

We were rehearsing at the Majestic Theater building in Grand Island. This was a dusty old theater with unpadded wooden seats that were solidly anchored to the concrete floor. These seats were hinged in the center so they folded up. This system, still used in plush theater seats today, allowed rows to be placed close together and therefore a greater number of seats in the house.

I was sitting in darkness at the extreme rear of the theater. This was a normal recital rehearsal, and my name would be called when it was time for me to perform. The eager ones, which were most of them, were either in the front row or in the wings waiting their turns. Miss Engstrom, our elder statesman of dance instructors, was wearing her usual purple velvet dance shorts. I had a good view of the stage from my vantage point, and could pretend to be a director. However, since I didn't wear my hated gold, wire-rimmed glasses except when my parents were around to supervise, I couldn't see the people onstage very well. Unfortunately, I could still hear the laborious speeding up and slowing of the music to accommodate the lack of talent of most of the dancers.

"Glenn Thompson! You're next!" This shattered me out of my daydreaming. I was seated in the direct center rear of the theater. When my name was called, I had to get to the stage very quickly to avoid being reprimanded for holding up the others. I had been thinking for some time of a method of eliminating the side trip to the aisle to get down to the stage. It was a personal challenge, especially in tap shoes with leather soles and heels. Mother wanted me develop better agility? She'd get it.

I planned to leap onto the top back edge of the hard wood seats and dash from seat back to seat back, arriving with a final graceful leap to the rail of the tiny orchestra pit. Then in one flowing move I would land between the footlights and onto the stage. I imagined the applause that would follow this feat.

As my grandkids would say, "Awesome!"

This time when my name was called I took a deep breath and started the dance of the seat backs for real. However, about two-thirds of the way down, my foot slipped from the top and dropped onto the back of an unfolded seat. It promptly folded and I came crashing down astride the narrow, wooden seat back.

I now knew what real pain was. I had thought I understood pain when a Shetland pony threw me off into a pile of rocks, or when I fell backwards off an eight-foot fence. People onstage called out, asking if I was all right as I lay writhing and moaning. Nobody actually walked up to find out. I couldn't answer. All my breath had been pushed out or sucked in. I wasn't sure which.

"Glenn Thompson, you're on."

Thankfully, when I didn't appear, the next dancer was called. "No matter what happens to me the rest of my life," I thought, "the pain and shock can't be worse than this." I was wrong.

At that time I had yet to see the window sticker prices on the new 1984 cars.

When I priced dealers in our area for the cost of that new Pontiac, I understood why they called our latest disease "sticker shock." Prices had inflated far beyond what I had realized. Of course this purchase was a major step-up from my '82 Nissan Stanza. It had cost around $7,500 for a fairly well-equipped automobile. Now I was looking at a slightly larger car in a two-year newer model for $15,000.

I preferred to buy from my friend Butch, the local Pontiac dealer, if he could be competitive on a trade. Although he told me he doubted that he could sell a Japanese car in our area, his trade-in price did turn out to be the best deal I could get.

After I bought the STE, the first time I pulled into my regular service station to fill with gas, the owner, Hap, beamed at me. "I'm sure glad you finally decided to buy an American-built car instead of one of those foreign things," he said.

"Sorry," I replied, "this is just another foreign-made car."

"Isn't this one of those sporty Pontiac Euro sedans?" he asked.

"Sure is," I answered. "Made in Canada."

Five years later I was hit by yet another dose of automobile price explosion. I remembered my father's oft repeated advice: "Whatever you do, never, ever pay more than three cents a pound for watermelon." His advice was to be patient. The price would always come down as the season progressed. More melons would be ripening all the time, until the melon grower had to sell at much lower prices.

We ate a lot of mushy watermelon, which often made me sick, but Dad never paid more than three cents a pound. I think I caught on to the moral of that when it came to automobile shopping. Never try to buy the very cheapest thing available or you may not be able to stomach it. I go, Yugo, we all go for PU-go.

Nevertheless, I had assumed at least some moderation in price increases on the new cars since quotas had been worked out with the Japanese. They had agreed to export a limited number of vehicles to the United States. Supposedly, this was an effort to hold down U.S. car prices, help preserve the American car manufacturers and the thousands of auto workers' jobs they represented. In a strange way I was reminded of an often quoted statement by Charles Wilson, U.S. Secretary of Defense during the 1950s: "What's good for General Motors is good for the USA."

Following the installation of quotas on imports, three things happened. First, the U.S. car industry promptly moved much of their assembly to other countries to reduce production costs. Mexico, for example, got plants from all three major manufacturers. There were no labor unions in Mexico. Nearly all the taillight assemblies for GM cars are now made in Mexico. These American plants are called *maquiladoras*.

In the mid 1980s a financial program on TV featured an interview which discussed the major advantages to both countries of a General Motors auto plant. This is not directly quoted but is very close to the answers given by a GM spokesman when he was asked about the wages being paid to the Mexican workforce.

"We, ah, pay, ah an, ah, average of about, that is the equivalent of, ah four dollars ah, mumble, mumble."

"Compared to the average wage for auto workers in the United States of twenty-some dollars an hour, including fringe benefits that's a tremendous savings, isn't it?" the interviewer asked.

"Yes. But it is far above the average pay in Mexico. We are very pleased with the quality of the work force here."

"You mean four dollars an hour is above the average industry pay on the Mexican border?"

"Oh, yes. Far above."

"You did mean that GM is paying four dollars per hour, didn't you?"

"Hmmph. Ah, well, ah, no. The pay is about four dollars per day. But that's far above the average wage here. We've got a huge waiting list of prospective employees!"

Labor cost savings are simply too great for car manufacturers to overlook. Quality seems to be comparable. It's difficult to criticize carmakers for doing what it takes to survive.

The second major change was the formation of company partnerships with Japanese firms, such as Ford with Mazda, Chevy with Toyota and Isuzu, and Chrysler with Mitsubishi. This shared technology probably helped U.S. industry more than it did Japanese. For one thing, the Japanese were far ahead of us in robotics and had more modern factories and machine tooling.

These marriages produced such cars as the Geo, Chevy Nova, Plymouth Colt and Conquest, and the perennial high-selling Ford Escort. Most of the popular Plymouth and Dodge minivans use Japanese-built engines. In fairness, Chrysler has since developed its own V-6s and now uses them in many models.

Many other makes and models include Japanese or other foreign-made components and technology with American styling added. The Taurus with a Yamaha engine is such a car.

Perhaps the most notoriety was reserved for the Dodge

Stealth. This excellent sports car was chosen as the pace vehicle for the 1991 Indianapolis 500, which is held each year on Memorial Day, a national holiday originally conceived to honor American military dead. Someone pointed out that the Dodge Stealth is about as American as baseball, the seventh of December, and Mama-san's apple pie. Only the name and a few styling tweaks distinguish it from a similar sports car made by its maker, Mitsubishi Motors of Japan. It was then decided that Indianapolis pace cars must be American-made.

Ford and General Motors have long had various ties to European manufacturers. Chrysler formed a major partnership with Renault, the French company, more or less by default. Chrysler bought out financially troubled American Motors, which had previously received a cash bailout in exchange for major percentage ownership by Renault. Renault cars were introduced to U.S. buyers under the AMC label which then became the Eagle division of Chrysler.

Still, the confusion and blurring of who makes what in the industry is remarkable. The car business has become internationalized to an extent beyond our imagination even a decade ago. Virtually no American car comes off the assembly line purely American today. Perhaps that's not necessarily bad over the long haul. Combining the technology and specialities of many different nations helps tie the world together economically. This interdependency may prove to be the ultimate key to world peace.

The third thing that happened to the car industry in the 1980s was that to avoid quotas, the Japanese began building plants in the United States, using our labor so that many of their cars could be considered U.S. makes. Honda's Ohio plant or Nissan's in Tennessee, for example, have proved that cars put together by American labor in modern factories are every bit as well built as the imports.

What I failed to understand while watching this senario unfold was why prices of U.S. cars during this period of quotas increased so dramatically. Overall inflation was moderate, so that couldn't be the reason. The 1980s appeared to be a good time for U.S. manufacturers to hold the line on prices and recapture some of the market lost to imports. Unfortunately, that didn't happen.

Since I had been generally satisfied with my Pontiac STE, four years later I was considering purchasing another one. There had been some improvements in the car. The interesting thing about the STE was that there were virtually no options. It had just about everything on it already. A sunroof could be added, if you were short enough to sit upright in the seat despite the loss of headroom, and leather seats were available as an option. That was about it.

My point is that we were comparing apples with apples as far as equipment on the car I already owned and a new one. The new Pontiac was still built on the same GM body that it had been four years earlier. The engine was basically the same, except that fuel injection had replaced the carburetor. Four-wheel drive replaced the front-wheel drive of my 1984 model, and there were a few other minor tweaks.

When I began looking at new cars, I landed astride the theater seats again. The pain of current prices numbed my body. The STE had gone up another $9,000 in four years! Since this car was quite popular, some of this cost increase was the old supply-and-demand factor at work. My best price was my car and $12,000, including those gimmicky factory rebates, dealer incentives, and so on.

We decided additional shopping was in order. I say "we" although Ardelle hates to shop for cars almost as much as I hate the endless women's clothing and shoe stores in the malls. However, I certainly don't want to choose a car on my own that she hates to drive. Her major consideration is that she does not like a vehicle that is clumsy to park or whose size strains the garage. She wants good passing power, safety, and excellent brakes. We always agree on the color and type of upholstery before we buy.

It took us another year of hem-hawing. After test driving

a number of models, the best deal I could find was on Chrysler New Yorker. This was definitely not a sports sedan like the Pontiac. However, it did have somewhat better acceleration than the STE, was larger, quieter, equally well appointed, and had a four-speed electronic automatic transmission. We referred to the Chrysler as our ''old peoples car,'' primarily because of the large digital readout of the speedometer and other car functions, and large, simple stereo system controls. The 1989 had conservative styling, a prestigeous name, good brakes, comfort, a soft ride, and surprisingly, very good fuel economy from its Mitsubishi engine.

Following an accident with the Chrysler, which I'll describe later, we once again traded cars and bought another foreign make—none other than the choice of the Washington, D.C. elected set—a 1992 Ford Crown Victoria.

The Crown Vic? An import? Heresy! True, there were some dramatic improvements in handling, electronics, a new engine, and a four-wheel disk brake package on the '92s, but it still seemed to be large, typical American sedan. As is happening with many cars, the Ford and Mercury Grand Marquis are being constructed with more than twenty-nine percent of the parts built in another country. Therefore, the cars are legally considered imported vehicles. See how the invasion of Japanese body snatchers is working?

# 12

## *Birds of a Feather*

ANNA MARIE IS A NEIGHBOR in our small town. She had volunteered to deliver food to housebound people through the Meals on Wheels program. This would appear to be not only a charitable bit of good-deed-doing, but relatively non-hazardous as well. It didn't work out that way for Anna Marie.

She stopped her Ford for her first delivery, got out of the car, and walked around to the opposite side and lifted out the food containers. By the time Anna Marie had rung the doorbell for her dinner delivery, her car suddenly appeared to be possessed. It leaped into reverse gear like a startled stallion and backed into the street. It jumped a curb, flattened a garbage can, and squashed a hedge. It miraculously missed parked cars, trees, and houses. In other words, it avoided anything strong enough to stop it.

Anna Marie heard the commotion and looked around just

in time to see her car back rapidly into another curb, ricochet off that, and bang into another. Then it settled into a general pattern of curb crunching, backwards in a large circle. Anna Marie watched, awestruck.

Another observer called the police. The officers decided there really wasn't much they could do short of ramming the car. They radioed for a wrecker. Nobody wanted to chance opening the door, as the car continued a rapid circle in reverse, for fear the door would knock them down and they would be run over by the angry car. The headstrong Ford continued its relentless backing and crunching.

"I never seen nothin' like that," a city employee volunteered.

Consultations began among law enforcement personnel, Floyd, the tow-truck driver, and other newly self-appointed resident experts.

"It's bound to run out of gas pretty quick," one of them opined.

"I just filled it yesterday!" Anna Marie moaned.

Finally one of the emergency crew decided this could get pretty serious if the car stopped bouncing around in circles and took off in some other direction, since a sizeable crowd of bystanders had assembled to witness the event.

So Floyd took an ax to it. He positioned himself near the center of the car's backward path, and on one close pass, made his daring matador move and smashed out the driver's side window. Then he ran along beside the vehicle, reached in, and managed to turn off the ignition switch.

This whole episode took about half an hour. Police chief Jackson, who had lost two of his patrol cars to this event, had joined the scene. He decided it would be well to take a statement from Anna Marie, who at that very moment appeared in the doorway of a nearby residence.

"Are you hurt?" he asked.

"No," she said, "I just started to worry about all those people who weren't going to get their meals on time, so I borrowed a phone and called them.''

Now, that is about as cool as most drivers of runaway cars get.

Our daughter Dawn now lives in Cleveland and is seldom ruffled by much of anything, except her five-year-old son. She can vouch for the ''loose cannon'' car similar to Anna Marie's from personal experience.

She was a newly licensed real estate agent and was calling on a family who had inquired about listing their home. It was raining. She decided this would be a very quick trip, so she parked in their driveway, a normal no-no for sales people.

Dawn went to the door and had just said hello to the couple, when they noticed her car was moving. Everybody ran outside, but it was too late. The car proceeded *up* the drive, ran into the garage, and knocked the building partially off its foundation.

''That's how you really make a good professional impression,'' she laughed, much later. ''You get there trying to create some good will and get a house listing, and end up knocking the thing down before you even get a chance to market it.'' This is the same daughter you may recall, who as a youngster demolished her bicycle after she ''hit a little bump.'' The little bump turned out to be a parked car. She really hasn't changed much.

This brings us to the great Audi unknown acceleration scare of the late 1980s. More than one hundred accidents reported with that German-made car were blamed on this strange condition. The problem always seemed to occur when a vehicle was pulling up for a stop or left running ''for just a minute,'' with the brake not set.

At first Audi tried to ignore the claims of faulty mechanicals. When sales fell following numerous lawsuits and publicity about the mysterious symptom, Audi ran a prodigious number of tests to try to duplicate the problem. They never did find anything wrong with the car. They finally redesigned the shift with an ''idiot proof'' mechanism that made it a bit more awkward to use, but which prevented lawsuits, if not the mechanical difficulty.

Then Ford was blamed for a similar "jumping into gear" problem, much like Anna Marie's. She, however, had the good sense to ignore a lawsuit, knowing the ultimate result is an increase in everyone's car insurance rates.

Next, charges were brought against a new electronic transmission in Chrysler automobiles that branded it the culprit of the dreaded unknown acceleration.

All these drivers couldn't have accidently left their automatic transmission in gear could they? Naw. The people who make a living from liability lawsuits say that is impossible. Chisel that in your nearest stone tablet as the final words from the almighty.

However, it does seem strange that ever since the automatic transmission has become a popular car option, there are many more garages that have a new splintered opening at the rear. Many more storefronts and plate glass windows have been crashed, and many more vehicles have gone off into the sunset, sans driver.

Who's to blame? Go figure. Is it the cars themselves? How many buggy pile ups do you suppose there were when horses were helping drivers? We all regard ourselves as expert drivers, but deep down we also know that most accidents are caused by poor or impaired judgment by the driver, rather than by mechanical problems.

A parallel example would be the aircraft industry, which does extensive examinations of every accident. A huge percentage of accidents are ultimately shown to be caused by "pilot error." Remember, pilots are highly skilled men and women at the peak of their abilities and experience. How much can be expected of us ordinary automobile drivers?

In any event, hundreds of tests by several manufacturers showed no mechanical problem that would validate "unknown acceleration." The other explanation—"the revengeful car syndrome"—logically can not apply to any vehicle. The exception, of course, is Dad's belligerent 1939 Chevy I told you about earlier; the car that burned down Ralph's garage. I'm just as positive that Chevy was possessed as all those other drivers are certain their automatic transmissions are somehow defective.

Do you remember the slogan used by Domino's Pizza, "We deliver in thirty minutes or your pizza is free"? It was a commercial that was criticized by the TV program "60 Minutes" and investigated by a congressional committee. I didn't think much about it at the time. Criticism centered around the fact that this promise caused speeding and careless driving by pizza deliverers. It was said that a large number of needless accidents resulted because of the advertising slogan.

One evening I was driving our Chrysler to take some friends out for dinner and we had to stop in a long lineup of cars. The point was brought home forcefully that deadline pizza delivery is indeed dangerous. A pizza delivery driver slammed into us. Apparently he did not even brake before hitting us. Perhaps he was busy reading the addresses on the boxed pizzas he was rushing to deliver.

Five cars were damaged, but ours, being the last in line, got the worst of it. The pizza driver, who was not hurt, ran to a nearby gas station and reported the accident. Very soon, dodging among the wreckage, the first emergency vehicle appeared. It was another pizza car. The three large pizzas were transferred to that driver and, with a colorful Dominos sleeve draped over his antenna, he sped away in hopes the company would not have to give away three free pizzas. Everything is a matter of priorities.

I understand Dominos no longer uses the slogan because of the number of lawsuits charging the company with encouraging reckless driving, which is diametrically opposed to wreckless driving. Perhaps their new slogan should be, "Faster to the Disaster."

Many unexpected things cause problems with cars. Each fall in recent years our town has been infested with huge flocks of crows. It started in the 1970s. This was about the time many of our area farmers were tearing out the mile-long shelter belts of large trees planted under government subsidy during the dust bowl days of the 1930s to prevent soil erosion. Removing the trees permited ditch-to-road planting of corn along the road and land-leveling of farms for gravity irrigation from canals.

With the invention of the center pivot irrigation system this process accelerated several times over. Trees were not compatible with the long pipe sections supported on towers and power-driven wheels. The entire pivot revolves around a centered water well and motorized pump. This made it possible to irrigate rough, hilly, marginal land and produce huge crops of surplus corn. The removal of many of the trees on the plains coupled with a large amount of grain spilled to the ground during mechanical harvesting methods had two effects on the crow population.

A much larger food source was easily available to them, attracting larger and larger flocks to the area. And, the loss of roosting places in rural area trees caused them to seek the only major remaining large trees, which were in the parks and residential areas of the towns. In particular, our town. National news called us "Crow City U.S.A."

The situation was merely humorous until we realized that the city seemed almost powerless to drive these huge, black birds away. They tried cracker shells, spotlights, and propane cannons, all to no avail. The crows roosted in the trees at night and went out to feed in the nearby cornfields by day. They were noisy, and the weight of the huge groups broke large branches from the trees. Worst of all, their dropping were everywhere, on sidewalks, homes, cars. This became a major health hazard. Moreover, bird droppings were ruining the paint on hundreds of vehicles.

It was foolhardy to visit friends during the evening without protective headgear or newspapers over your head. Some good

hosts stood beneath the roof of their porches and threw firecrackers into the yard to keep the birds away while the guests were arriving. The evening trees looked like a scene from Alfred Hitchcock's movie adaptation of Daphne DeMaurier's, *The Birds*. In our town, many people began to wonder if it might turn into the same ending, with the crows winning.

The local gun club volunteered its members to help correct the problem. They agreed to do the work at no charge, except for the cost of reloaded shotgun shells. They offered to use their particular skills and accuracy until enough of the black avengers were killed to get the message across to the rest. It seemed to be the safest solution, albeit a desperate one.

Then the trouble began. Because of the publicity nationwide, bird lovers (who didn't have to live here) began objecting to killing the crows. Medical personnel thought the dead carcasses, judging from the volume of crows in the city each night, might be left to lay too long before the next day's clean-up and could pose a health hazard. Then someone asked the city council about liability. What if a well-meaning gun club member accidently shot off an electric cable in the older section of town or shot someone's pet cat ensconced in a tree? What if there should be a loss of human life?

It was decided that the gun club members could not be allowed to shoot crows within the city limits. During the day, the crows were widely spread over hundreds of square miles, so hunting them with any degree of success was impossible. Furthermore, even though crows are pretty smart birds, they certainly would not associate any deaths among their numbers out in the country with their roosting places in town. In the meantime the crows had nearly destroyed the trees in an old, beautiful park, and were working on the residential district. The public demanded action.

The city decided that there would be much less liability if their own employees were used. So every evening there was a tremendous banging as shotgun-wielding city employees, not really trained for this sort of armed attack, blasted at the crows. The results of the war were not known until the crows continued on their migration south. Then, like Saddam Hussein, the city simply declared a victory and called back the troops. The final crow body count divided into the amount of overtime wages, gas for city vehicles, and shotgun shells, showed a cost of $4.38 per dead crow.

I thought perhaps a less expensive solution would be a marketing plan to bring in tourists to view the crows. Can't you envision the magazine or newspaper ads?

SEE THE WORLD'S LARGEST CONGREGATION
OF WILD BIRDS!

Up close sightings guaranteed or your money back. Experience Nature in the raw! Guides available for modest fees.

(A shrewd way to use the city employees more profitably).

Another possible approach: ''During the late fall and early winter months, when birding slows in northern climates, you now have the opportunity to record a sighting of the rare White Spotted Crow. Birding scopes and binoculars available

for rental.'' (Actually any crow not sitting on the uppermost branches among the tightly packed flocks was certain to be white spotted.)

Or: ''Bed and Breakfast available near crow viewing sites. Experience the thunderous flapping of thousands of wings! Hear the raucous calling and crepitations of these delightful winged specimens. Best of all, you can capture one for your very own with the help of our trained experts and purchase a portable cage to take it home with you! Imagine the pleasure you will experience in teaching this intelligent crow to talk.

Bird food not required. Eats anything.'' (A cottage industry is born!)

My oldest grandson, Adam, was about three years old at the time of the crow invasion, yet he already knew of one problem with automobiles that needed a solution. He thought it had been invented when he saw a new device I had purchased. He was fascinated by the chirping noises made by my new radar detector.

After forty-some years of driving, I had received my first ticket for speeding a few weeks earlier, hence the purchase. I didn't get into the details with Adam. When it was first turned on, the detector went through a series of self checks which included loud cheeps. Adam was entranced.

''What's that, Grandpa?'' he asked. ''It sounds like a bird.''

''That's what it is,'' I told him in typical grandfatherly double talk. ''It's my new bird detector.'' After turning it on and off a couple more times at his request, we drove farther down the road without any more comment.

Adam's father, our son-in-law, Al, is a very good shot. After he had about all the destruction he could take from the nightly crow invasion, he had stepped outside his back door, taken two blasts with his shotgun into the large trees in his yard, and killed eighteen crows. Many residents had begun taking similar measures to stop the spread of contamination the birds were inflicting on everything left outside. This most certainly included the huge white stains on automobiles. Obviously, this had impressed Adam.

When he returned home after our car ride, his folks asked him what he had been doing when he was with grandpa.

He replied, ''Grandpa showed me his new bird detector.''

''His what?'' his mother asked, not knowing we had bought the radar device. ''What's it for?''

''The lights go on and it cheeps like a bird. Then it gets quiet, and if crows fly over that are going to crap on Grandpa's new car, it makes bird noises and scares them away.''

Now if it could only work with sparrows, starlings, and

pigeons too. . . .

Perhaps new devices will soon be invented to prevent the other unfortunate problems associated with driving, such as rear-end collisions and runaway cars. Radar with automatic braking, or some advanced derivative, may be installed on automobiles to lessen the danger of accidents.

However, some of the electronic devices already in use need refinement. Take the garage door opener. Dr. Bob and his wife, Dorothy, are like most of us. Often they don't leave quite at their scheduled departure time for a trip. Dr. Bob got held up slightly, and since they were running late, Dorothy used the garage door opener to raise the door and help speed things up. Suddenly she remembered an important item she had forgotten to bring along. She laid the opener on the seat of the car and dashed back into the house just as Dr. Bob was exiting.

"What did you forget now? Come on, hurry up or we'll never make it on time." He went into the open garage and started the car.

Dorothy ran back out of the house and jumped into the car, and they began backing rapidly out of the garage.

CRASH!! SCREECH!! RIP!!

"What in hell is happening?" Dr. Bob demanded. Then it became obvious to him that his garage door had come to a scraping, crunching rest on the roof of his car.

"Must have been an airplane triggered the thing," he surmised in disgust as he surveyed the damage to the car roof and the garage door.

"Must have been," Dorothy agreed, while stealthily sliding the opener she had just sat on toward the center of the front seat.

Don't worry, improvements and electronic gee-whizzes are arriving at breakneck speed. If only we can afford to buy them, we'll be ready for the next century. Just remember, cars will always get to you financially. If you don't believe it, you're still not watching your wallet, your credit cards, and your checkbook for the telltale signs of automobilitis.

The question is, what other expenditure produces such a sense of gratification as a new car? Of course, later will come the wild swings of emotion between one repair expense and the next, or between repeated trips to the dealership to get things corrected. This is called the annoyance factor. Fortunately, we Americans have very short memories of annoyances, and prefer to focus on the long-range picture. Unfortunately, there we find the always-certain yearly vehicle taxes, parking expenses, wheel taxes, tolls, routine maintenance, inspections, drivers license exams, and the insidious expense—depreciation. We tend to forget that until it's time to trade for another new car. It's then that we become aware of how much money has really been lost.

Nominate any other financial disaster and it's doubtful that over the long term it can measure up to the cost of owning an automobile. On the other hand, we all need to make a few ridiculous investments somewhere along life's highway. In retrospect, our vehicles have provided some of the most memorable (frustrating, humorous, enjoyable, proud) events in our lifetimes. They have an inestimable value of their own. Maybe our car purchases really are worth it.

Glenn E. Thompson is a native Nebraskan and a graduate of the University of Nebraska at Kearney. At various times he has been a newspaper editor, radio announcer and program director, insurance salesman, audio-visual producer, advertising producer, free-lance writer, and member of the speakers' bureau of the Nebraska Humanities Council.

Thompson is currently working on a history of World War II German POW camps for the Phelps County (Nebraska) Historical Society and an audio children's book. Thompson and his wife of forty-one years have three married daughters and seven grandchildren.